Student Activity
Part I

THE RABBIS' BIBLE

FOR VOLUME ONE:

TORAH

Morris J. Sugarman

Behrman House, Inc.
Publishers

ACKNOWLEDGMENTS

I am deeply grateful to a number of people who have helped me in the preparation of this workbook: Bonita Weisman, managing editor of Behrman House, who supervised its production — her first such project — with so large a degree of competence, conscientiousness, and enthusiasm; Karen Rossel, whose reading of the original manuscript contributed so significantly to its improvement; and Mrs. Bettie Reynolds, who typed the manuscript with unfailing professionalism and constant good cheer.

And I am especially grateful to Seymour Rossel, vice-president of Behrman House, who has worked with me through every stage of this project, and who has been one of the main reasons why I have found writing for Behrman House so rewarding, and so much fun.

Book designed and illustrated by Marvin Friedman

ISBN: 0-87441-319-2

This asterisk * appears before exercises
for which answers can be found in the Answer Key,
pages 103–108.

To Lori Sue, with love and hope.

A.

B.

C.

D.

E.

F.

1 GENESIS [1-3]
CREATION

Bible Review

SCENES OF THE CREATION*

The drawings below show steps in the creation of the universe, as they are described in this chapter. In the space at the top of each drawing, write the name of the day on which that particular scene took place. Sometimes a number of things were created on the same day; therefore, two or more scenes may refer to that day. Remember—the Sabbath is one of the days of creation. The text states: "And on the seventh day God ended His work." And Midrash [8] explains: "He created rest on the Sabbath, which is not merely the absence of work."

G.

H.

I.

J.

TRUE OR FALSE?*

Check T if true; F if false.

1. Darkness existed before light. T [ ] F [ ]

2. The lights in the heavens were created for one purpose: to separate the day from the night. T [ ] F [ ]

3. Because human beings were made in the image of God, the sixth day was reserved just for the creation of man and woman. T [ ] F [ ]

4. Grass and plants, fruit trees and birds, fish and insects, and beasts and human beings have the following things in common: (a) they are God's creations;   (b) they are alive;   (c) they have the means of reproducing themselves. T [ ] F [ ]

5. If Adam and Eve had not disobeyed God's command, they would have lived forever. T [ ] F [ ]

6. All of God's creations were completed in six days. T [ ] F [ ]

7. The earth brought forth many kinds of fruit trees in order to feed the animals that God had created. T [ ] F [ ]

8. Although God drove Adam and Eve from the Garden of Eden in punishment for their disobedience, He continued to watch over them, and provide for them. T [ ] F [ ]

9. The sun, moon, and stars marked the days, the years, and the various seasons. T [ ] F [ ]

10. Before the creation of heaven and earth the world was nothing but a mass of fire. T [ ] F [ ]

11. Before eating from the Tree of Knowledge, Adam and Eve did not have free will. T [ ] F [ ]

12. Adam gave names to all of the birds and beasts of the field. T [ ] F [ ]

Each of the five scrambled words below plays an important part in the story of Adam and Eve in the Garden of Eden. Unscramble them. Write the words in the boxes that follow. Then, unscramble the ten circled letters to make a word that sums up the outcome of this story.

1. eret

2. rituf

3. netresp

4. gwekolend

5. mehas

Midrash Review

Each of the following statements can be completed by several facts or ideas that appear in the Midrash. Circle the letter before the fact or idea that does *not* belong. (For example, Eve was   (a) created after Adam (b) blessed by God   (c) called the mother of all living   (d) angry because Adam was created first   (e) punished for her disobedience by being expelled from the Garden of Eden)

1. God saw that what He created "was good" because   (a) He had created other worlds that had displeased Him   (b) the Torah, the sacred Law, was a crucial factor in the creation of this world   (c) God created this world along lines of order, plan, and purpose   (d) human beings were given the ability to recognize good and evil   (e) human beings were forced to obey God's laws in this world

2. The Midrash explains that human beings might have been created last so that   (a) everything would be ready for us   (b) we would not be able to witness the process of creation   (c) we might learn modesty and humility   (d) our first experience would be to celebrate the Sabbath

3. The Sabbath   (a) was the day on which rest was created   (b) signifies a sense of spiritual renewal   (c) celebrates the joy of life   (d) was God's favorite achievement   (e) means more than just not working or taking it easy

4. According to the Midrash,   (a) Eve's union with Adam was blessed and made holy by God   (b) Eve was jealous of the fact that Adam was created first   (c) Adam lied to Eve (or stretched the truth a bit) to shield her from the temptation of disobeying the Lord's command   (d) the serpent talked Eve into eating the forbidden fruit by showing her that Adam did not tell her the truth   (e) the serpent was originally the king of the animals   (f) the serpent deliberately plotted to cause trouble between human beings and God

5. The values highlighted in the Midrashim of this chapter include   (a) the sanctity of life   (b) the equality of all people   (c) the evil of riches   (d) the fact that in unity there is strength and security   (e) the need for both justice and mercy in the world

LOOKING FOR UNDERSTANDING

The Midrash helps us understand the Bible in many ways—through stories, explanations, and interpretations. In your own words, sum up what the Midrash reveals about each of the following:

1. The institution of marriage

_____

_____

_____

2. The value of life

_____

_____

_____

4

3. Justice and mercy

_____

_____

_____

4. Individuality

_____

_____

_____

5. Equality

_____

_____

_____

6. Freedom of choice

_____

_____

_____

7. Unity and peace

_____

_____

_____

Summing Up

THE MEANING OF THE SABBATH

The Sabbath is among the most ancient, and the holiest, of Jewish traditions. The Bible speaks of it as part of the Creation itself. It has also been widely misunderstood. Many people think Sabbath rest means a time to lounge around and do nothing, a time to go to the movies, to the beach, or to a ball game. Such people become very impatient when they are told about the various laws and customs that they are supposed to observe on the Sabbath, and complain, "Instead of being a time to relax, the Sabbath is just a bunch of do's and don'ts. You can't do this, and you can't to that, and you *must* do something else. That's not my idea of taking it easy." How would you reply to these complaints? Try answering in the space below. (Hint: See the text, Midrash [8], and use your own ideas and experiences.)

GENESIS [4-11]
CAIN AND ABEL; NOAH

Bible Review

WHO (OR WHAT) AM I?*

This chapter discusses people, places, events, and objects. Using the statements below, tell who, or what, is being described.

1. I have been called "colorful" and even "beautiful" by many, and I served as a symbol of God's promise to all humanity that He would never again destroy the earth because of people's evil.

   _____

2. The motto of those who built me could have been "The sky's the limit!"_____

3. I was ignored—you might even say rejected—and this greatly angered the person who brought me. _____

4. I was the youngest of three, but I had the largest impact upon the future because of my descendants. _____

5. After being cooped up for so long, it was a pleasure to find a new home. You could say that I was the first to abandon ship, but my shipmates thought my disappearance was a hopeful sign.

   _____

6. I was used not to brand a murderer, but to protect him.

   _____

7. My life-style and values were different from those of everyone else. I stood apart from the majority, and lived to tell about it.

   _____

8. I was the victim of one of the most powerful human emotions: jealousy. _____

9. Maybe I wasn't much to look at, but I was solidly built, and did what I was supposed to do. Future generations would think of me as a lifesaver. _____

10. I was the instrument of destruction which the Lord set loose upon a world "filled with corruption and violence." _____

WHAT THE TORAH SAYS*

In each of the statements that follow, circle the letter before the one ending that *exactly*—not just possibly—completes the idea correctly.

1. The tower builders of Babel   (a) were hard workers   (b) were excellent craftspeople   (c) enjoyed each other's company   (d) were finally scattered all over the world   (e) were young, strong, enthusiastic people

2. Noah could be described as   (a) a good father   (b) a devoted husband   (c) a true individual whose ideas about life were opposite to those of the majority   (d) a humble man, who wondered why he, of all people, had been chosen to be saved   (e) a compassionate man, who grieved for those who perished in the flood, despite their wickedness

3. One of the lessons learned from the story of Cain and Abel is that   (a) God loved Abel more than Cain   (b) God regarded murder as a serious crime, to be punished severely   (c) God cherished the work of tending sheep more than that of tilling the soil   (d) if a person is born with a killer instinct, sooner or later he or she will take a life   (e) jealousy always leads to sorrow and tragedy

4. An important teaching contained in the story of the Tower of Babel is that   (a) unity can be a source of great strength   (b) if

people cannot understand each others' languages, they will find it difficult, if not impossible, to work together   (c) if all people speak a single language and consider themselves united ("one people") they will rebel against God Himself   (d) as long as people remain scattered over the face of the earth, speaking different languages, practicing different customs, God can feel safe and secure

5. The rainbow, symbol of God's covenant, stands for   (a) God's love of many colors   (b) God's love of beauty   (c) the fact that God's miracles could only be seen at a great distance   (d) God's commitment to keep His promise to Noah and to all the generations to follow   (e) God's wish that Noah live with an easy mind, free from fear of future floods

6. God's statement to Cain after taking no notice of his offering ("If you do right, you shall be happy, but if you do not do right, sin lies in wait at the door.") contains the idea that   (a) God is all-powerful   (b) God is all-knowing   (c) to disobey the Lord is to invite punishment   (d) God is always willing to give a person a second chance   (e) people have free will—the ability to know, and to choose between, good and evil—and are, therefore, responsible for their own actions

7. Adam and Eve, Cain, and the builders of the Tower of Babel all   (a) disobeyed God's commands   (b) had little regard for human life   (c) knew the sorrow of exile in one form or another as punishment for what they had done   (d) wanted to rebel against God and challenge His power   (e) sought forgiveness for what they had done

8. The three stories that are told in this chapter make the common point that   (a) people are always going to be corrupt—it is human nature   (b) in certain circumstances, anyone, like Cain, might murder   (c) in every generation, there is one righteous person, such as Noah, who can save humanity   (d) God is always with us—actively involved in what we do, and concerned with the way we live our lives

BETWEEN THE LINES*

The Bible covers a great deal of ground by telling us things in a short and factual way. The purpose of this exercise is to figure out who might have said what to whom—between the lines, using what you know and understand of the stories. Adam and Eve, for example, must have talked to each other about something, between the time that they were driven from the Garden of Eden and the birth of their sons. And during the days and weeks and months that they were on board the ark, Noah's family must have had many discussions about when, and even whether, they would ever see dry land again, and what the future would be like. Match the statements, in the right column, with the characters who might have made them, in the left column. Make your choice by placing the numbers showing who is speaking to whom in the blank spaces beside the statements that they might have made.

1. Abel to Cain

_____ What people say about you is true. You're crazy! The weirdest person I have ever met! I'm not talking about this mess of wood-work you've been puttering around with for so long—everyone is entitled to have a hobby. What bothers me is that you are so sure that you're right and the whole world is wrong. You have no respect for the attitudes and life-styles of your neighbors. According to you, your way is the only way. What nerve! What conceit!

2. Noah to one of his sons

_____ Look, I know what you're think-ing, but remember—two wrongs don't make a right. I am a marked man for life. If you kill me, you will become one, too, only worse.

3. A neighbor of Noah to Noah

_____ For Heaven's sake, stop mumbling and speak up! I can't understand a word you're saying. We will never finish at this rate!

4. Cain to a stranger he has met

_____ Why are you angry with me? Did I do anything to you? Was any of this my fault? I just did the best I could. I made no judgment. Be-sides, it's not as though you haven't been given another chance. You were told what you have to do, in no uncertain terms.

5. Adam to Eve   ____ What this teaches us is that God not only binds us to the rule of law; He binds himself, as well. He has given us His word, and this is His way of telling us that He will keep it—for all time.

6. One citizen of Babel to another   ____ In a way, it's like history repeating itself. First we were punished by being driven into exile, and now the same thing has happened to our firstborn.

Midrash Review

THE REASONS WHY

The stories in this chapter did not take place in a vacuum; everything that happened had a reason, which the Midrash sets forth and explains. According to the interpretations of the Midrash, complete the sentences below.

1. God took notice of Abel's offering, but not Cain's because

_____

_____

2. Cain's words, "am I my brother's keeper," were rejected by the Lord because _____

_____

3. Noah labored over the ark for so long (it took 125 years to build) because_____

_____

4. After enduring people's arrogance, rebelliousness, and idol-worship for many years, God finally decided to punish them because

_____

_____

5. King Nimrod and his subjects decided to build a tower "so high that it will reach the heaven" because _____

_____

6. Their plan was foiled, and work on the tower came to a halt because_____

_____

A Dutch engraving from about 1700 showing how one artist imagined Noah's Ark was built.

LOOKING FOR UNDERSTANDING

The Midrash often explains passages of the Bible in terms of social and moral values. Briefly tell what attitudes and values, good and bad, you find in the following quotations from the Midrash:

1. " 'I made you in My image,' God replied, 'with a brain and a soul. Were I to direct your every act, you would be no more than a puppet.' " Midrash [2]

2. "God patiently overlooked transgression and idolatry, but when men robbed the poor, the orphan and the widow, corrupted justice and shed innocent blood, God determined to punish them." Midrash [6]

3. "Make an ark of gopher wood, but do not hasten as you build it; perchance the people will repent and be saved." Midrash [6]

4. "Abel selected the best of his flocks, but Cain offered that which was left from his own meal." Midrash [1]

5. "Let us build a city . . . and a tower so high that it will reach the heaven. We shall inscribe our names on its bricks and be remembered forever." Midrash [8]

6. "Men were so prosperous that they no longer put their trust in Him." Midrash [8]

7. "Why did God choose to dwell in heaven, while to us is given the earth?" Midrash [8]

8. "If a man fell to his death, no one mourned; but if a brick dropped, the workmen wailed and tore their hair, because it would take a year to replace it." Midrash [8]

Summing Up

A CIRCLE OF JEWISH RESPONSIBILITY

The individual Jew, no less than the community, must act as a "brother's keeper." The circle that follows shows key areas of Jewish need. Fill in the spaces below each title with your own briefly stated ideas of how you might help.

If you feel some areas are more important than others, let your answers show this (e.g., one space might be full of ideas; another practically empty); it will give you a pretty clear picture of where your Jewish values lie.

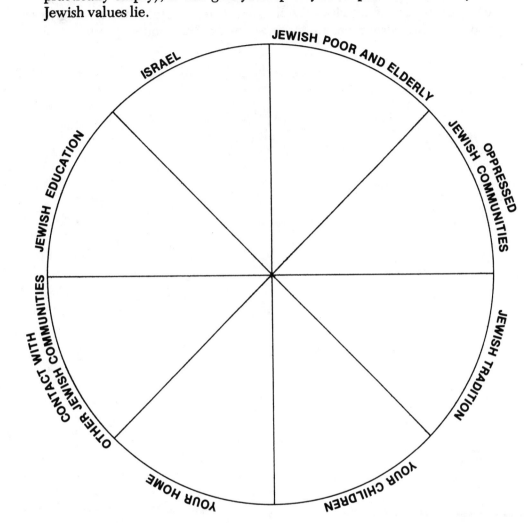

MY BROTHER'S KEEPER

In addition to the interpretation given in Midrash [2], the idea of "my brother's keeper" has become a value of central importance in Jewish tradition: *Kol Yisrael Arevim Zeh Ba-Zeh*, "All of Israel (or, All Jews) are responsible for one another," involved with other Jews, committed to their well-being.

In the space below, discuss some of the ways in which your Jewish community expresses the ideals of acting as our "brother's keeper," in terms of its various activities. Your rabbi, teacher, and parents can give you valuable information and insights; use them as resource people.

Bible Review

*FINDING THE FACTS**

Fill in the blank spaces below with the correct facts, all of which appear in the biblical text.

Terah, his son Abram, _____, Abram's wife, and
_____, Abram's nephew, set out from
_____ of the _____ to go to
_____. However, they settled in the city of
_____ until the death of Terah. Shortly thereafter, the Lord commanded Abram to continue his journey to the land where He would make of Abram's descendants a great _____. Abram's household set forth, finally arriving in the city of _____, where Abram built an _____ to the Lord. Abram prospered, but he was grieved that _____ broke out between his shepherds and those of his nephew. Because he wished to preserve close family ties, he pleaded with Lot to _____ from him, offering Lot first choice of the land that lay before them. Lot chose the plain of the _____ because its land was _____, and set up his household in the city of Sodom, already known for its _____ against the Lord. Abram, in accordance with God's command, _____ throughout the land, finally settling beside the oaks of _____

in _____. He later proved his devotion to his nephew, as well as his own courage and resourcefulness, by defeating the armies of the _____ _____, who had taken Lot prisoner. When offered a reward by the king of the city where Lot lived, Abram refused to accept anything, but did ask that those who fought with him receive their _____. Afterward, when God appeared in a vision to Abram, Abram complained that he was _____, and that as a result, his servant _____ would be his heir. The Lord promised Abram that his heir would be one _____ to him, and that his descendants would be as numerous as the _____. And after revealing glimpses of the future, God forged a _____ with Abram, promising to give the land to his descendants. Finally, Sarai, remaining childless, gave her maid _____ in marriage to Abram. And from this marriage, Abram fathered _____, his firstborn son, when he was eighty-six years old.

MAP STUDY: ABRAM'S JOURNEYS*

Abram and the members of his household were a very well-traveled group of people, especially for the times in which they lived. The map below is of the Middle East today. The numbers on the map represent the various ancient locations mentioned in the accounts of Abram's journeys, and are described in the statements (with matching numbers) that follow. Write the name of each ancient location next to its number on the map. (At times, ancient and modern names are the same.)

1. The town in which Abram built his first altar to God in the land of Canaan.

2. The city, usually thought of as Abram's birthplace, from which Terah and his family originally emigrated.

3. The country whose richness of soil was compared to "the garden of the Lord" and about which God informed Abram that his "descendants shall be strangers, . . . enslaved and oppressed for four hundred years." (By the way, Abram and his family fled to

18

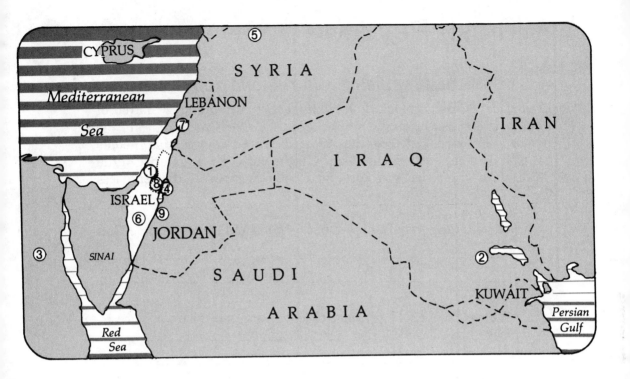

that country, for a period of time, when Canaan was besieged by famine.)

4. The body of water where the armies of the four kings joined to wage war against Sodom, Gomorrah, and their neighbors.

5. The city in which Terah and Abram settled on their way to Canaan (where Terah ultimately died).

6. The area in Canaan where Abram journeyed after building his first altar in that land.

7. The site of the battle between the servants of Abram and the armies of the four kings.

8. The place where Abram settled (including the specific location and the city of which it was a part), after his separation from Lot.

9. The area chosen by Lot, at Abram's request, after the quarrels that broke out between their shepherds.

Midrash Review

IDOL WORSHIP AND THE ONE GOD

The Midrash spends much time talking about Abram's great hatred of idol worship, and his passionate belief in the One God. What are the major differences between the assorted graven images that people worshiped then, and the One God? On the basis of the material in the Midrash, and of what you know and believe, complete the sentences below.

1. Whereas idols were fashioned out of wood and stone, the One God

   _____

   _____

2. Whereas idols could be seen, touched, and moved from place to place, the One God _____

   _____

3. Whereas idols could be broken, bent or completely destroyed, the One God _____

   _____

4. Whereas idols were considered to be "specialists," with each god in charge of a specific area (e.g., the sun god, the moon god, the god of the sea), the One God _____

   _____

5. Whereas idols, in the eyes of those who worshiped them, were mostly concerned with ritual and sacrificial offering, the One God

   _____

   _____

LOOKING FOR UNDERSTANDING

The Midrash does a lot of searching between the lines in this chapter—explaining, interpreting, spelling out the reasons behind the dramatic events that are told in the biblical text. Using the Midrash as your source, try to answer the following questions.

1. Why did Nimrod wish to kill Abram?

_____

_____

_____

2. Why did Abram reject the moon, the stars, and finally, the sun as gods, and what reasoning led him to the conclusion that there was but One God?

_____

_____

_____

_____

3. What arguments did Abram use to prove that the idols that everyone worshiped were not gods?

_____

_____

_____

4. Why did God allow Nimrod to continue to persecute Abram and his family?

_____

_____

_____

5. What values caused Abram to reject the life-style of Aramnaharaim in favor of that of Shechem?

_____

_____

_____

_____

6. Why was Abram described as a person who "created souls"?

_____

_____

_____

7. What, in your opinion, does the following statement mean? "Only he who knows the land can possess it." Midrash [6]

_____

_____

_____

8. Which values, held and cherished by Abram, moved him to say to Lot, "Kinsman, let us separate and go each his way"?

_____

_____

_____

9. What did the fiery furnace and the torch stand for?

_____

_____

_____

10. How would you define the meaning of "a light unto the nations"?

_____

_____

_____

Summing Up

A CHARACTER SKETCH OF ABRAM

The statements below are descriptions of Abram, drawn from the text and the Midrash. In the spaces that follow, write what you think each description shows about his attitudes, his values, and his outlook on life. Together, they should yield a rounded and interesting character sketch of Abram. (For example, a description: "Joe gives money to everyone who approaches him with a hard luck story!" Possible character analysis: "Joe is a generous man" or "Money means very little to Joe; people are his first concern.")

1. Abram's rejection of idol worship.

2. Abram's deliberate mocking of those who worshiped idols, including Terah, his father.

3. Abram's pulling up roots in Haran, and setting out for Canaan—a land he had never seen.

4. Abram's ability to "create souls."

5. Abram's rejection of the life-style of Aramnaharaim, and his admiration of the way people lived in Shechem.

6. Abram's rescue of Lot, and the manner in which he refused the reward offered him by the king of Sodom.

7. Abram's response to the quarrels that arose between his and Lot's shepherds.

GENESIS [17-21]
SODOM AND GOMORRAH

Bible Review

TRUE OR FALSE?*

1. God changed the names Abram and Sarai to Abraham and Sarah, as a way of expressing His special affection for them.
T [   ]   F [   ]

2. Because God's covenant was with the children of Isaac, Ishmael's descendants could not become a great nation.   T [   ]   F [   ]

3. At different times, Abraham and Sarah both laughed at the prediction that they would have a son in their old age.
T [   ]   F [   ]

4. Sarah was personally scolded by the Lord for showing so little faith in His promise that she would give birth to a son.   T [   ]   F [   ]

5. The visit of the three strangers showed that hospitality was a value that Abraham cherished and practiced.   T [   ]   F [   ]

6. The value of hospitality was also cherished and practiced by Lot.   T [   ]   F [   ]

7. The Lord revealed His plans for destroying Sodom and Gomorrah to Abraham because He wanted to see if this man with whom He had forged a sacred covenant was capable of compassion.
T [   ]   F [   ]

8. The story of Sodom and Gomorrah showed the importance that God placed upon the quality of righteousness.   T [   ]   F [   ]

9. This story further showed that God's ways must never be questioned, for once He made a judgment, it was firm, fixed, and final. T [   ] F [   ]

10. God's judgment of Sodom and Gomorrah was made only after He Himself had gone down to witness the evil within the cities. T [   ] F [   ]

LOOKING FOR UNDERSTANDING

Support the following general statements with one or more specific references to, or quotations from, the text.

1. Abraham and Sarah had moments of doubt about God's promise to provide them with a son in their old age. _____

_____

_____

2. Both Abraham and Lot cherished, and expressed, the value of hospitality. _____

_____

_____

3. Though the Lord forged His covenant with Abraham, Isaac, and their descendants, He was actively concerned with the lives of other peoples, as well. _____

_____

_____

4. Abraham possessed qualities of great courage and deep compassion.

_____

_____

5. God proved that He had not only the power to create and destroy, but also the capacity to listen. _____

_____

_____

6. The story of Sodom and Gomorrah points up the Lord's overriding concern with morality, justice, and compassion; that is, the way that people behave toward one another. _____

_____

_____

7. Abraham's unique relationship with God was based not upon special privilege, but upon special responsibility. _____

_____

_____

Midrash Review

FROM WHAT YOU KNOW . . .

What do the following statements and actions tell you about God's nature?

1. God's rebuke of Abraham for driving the idolator from his home. Midrash [1]

_____

_____

_____

2. God's reasons for destroying Sodom and Gomorrah. Midrash [3]

_____

_____

_____

3. God's descending to see how Sodom and Gomorrah had sinned. Midrash [2]

_____

_____

_____

4. God's promise to treat His people with compassion. Midrash [1]

_____

_____

_____

5. The Lord's willingness to listen and respond to Abraham's pleas for compassion toward the citizens of Sodom and Gomorrah. Midrash [4]

_____

_____

_____

A RECIPE FOR DESTRUCTION*

The following terms were among the main ingredients in the corruption and degradation of Sodom and Gomorrah. Unscramble the letters and, when necessary, the word order, to create a recipe for God's destruction of these two cities. (Examples: **fragt** = graft; **tisoyec a prucort** = society a corrupt = a corrupt society)

1. **deger** =

2. **nelvoeci** =

3. **grentrass trulecy ot** =

4. **het seproonips opro fo** =

5. **wals nustuj** =

Summing Up

ABRAHAM'S JOURNAL*

Imagine that Abraham kept a journal of his experiences, in which he recorded his thoughts, his feelings, and his responses. Match each journal note in the right column with the experience in the left column to which it refers. This journal includes events and interpretations set forth in the texts and midrashim of both chapters 3 and 4.

1. The birth of Ishmael

_____ To me, family harmony is more important than land, money, or property; it was with this in mind that I made the offer that I did.

2. The renaming of Abram and Sarai to Abraham and Sarah; and God's command of circumcision as "a token of the covenant" between the Lord and Abraham and his descendants

_____ I didn't know what to say to Him, or how to answer Him. But I understand fully why she found it so difficult to have faith in a prediction that flies in the face of reality, of physical logic as we have come to know it.

3. The birth of Isaac

_____ I am truly ashamed of myself, allowing my hatred of idolatry to violate values of home and hospitality that I have held dear all of my life.

4. The vision of the smoking furnace and the flaming torch

_____ It is truly a "blessed event"—even though it is not as I had imagined, or hoped, it would be. But at eighty-six years of age, I am old enough, and maybe wise enough, to realize that life is not always a series of made-to-order happy endings.

5. Abraham's pleading with God to spare Sodom for the sake of even ten righteous citizens, if they could be found

_____ I guess I could be called a disrespectful son and highly destructive. But I did what I did to make my father see, to make him understand.

6. Sarah's laughter at the prediction of one of the guests that "next year at this season. . .[she] shall have a son"

_____ Sure it is a gamble, a venture into the unknown; He has asked a great deal—and promised a great deal more. For what He has asked of me is to leave my home. And what He has promised, in return, is nothing less than a glowing future.

7. Abram's offering Lot his choice of land after the conflict that erupted between their shepherds

_____ One is never too old, I guess. After nearly a century of being known one way, to have to get used to being known another; and then, of course, there was the physical change, with all of the pain that went with it.

8. God's rebuke of Abraham for casting the elderly pagan from his home for refusing to reject his cherished graven image

_____ The nerve, people might say, the utter gall of my presuming to bargain with God. Maybe so, but I did what I had to—in the name of my own values and commitment. And the fact that He *did* listen, that He *did* allow Himself to bargain, points up His compassion, and above all, His belief in our ability to change for the better.

9. God's command to Abram to leave his country, his kin, and his father's house "and go to the land that I will show you; and I will make of you a great nation"

_____ Incredible; a total miracle; a gift of laughter that proves beyond a doubt that nothing is impossible for the Lord.

10. Abram's smashing of Terah's idols

_____ I confess, these two symbols filled me with dread—but with comfort, too, in a strange way. They pointed to suffering in the future, but they also expressed a commitment to justice and moral enlightenment. If that is the mission of my children's children, so be it!

CORRUPTION THEN AND NOW

Sodom and Gomorrah were not cities from distant planets; rather, they stood for the worst impulses of individuals and whole societies—human corruption in the extreme. The following statements, taken from Midrash [3], describe elements of the corruption that existed in Sodom and Gomorrah. In the spaces below, fill in what you believe to be examples of these corrupt elements at work today.

1. "As their wealth grew, so did their greed."

2. " 'We do not wish strangers among us,' they said. 'They come here to take something from us.' Any traveler who strayed into their cities was made to regret that he had come."

3. "They did not look after widows and orphans, though they hungered."

4. "They devised evil each against his fellow."

5. "And in their laws [they] favored the rich over the poor."

HEBREW MEANINGS

Find the Hebrew meanings of the following names and in a sentence or two, discuss what you think they signify.

1. Abraham

2. Sarah

3. Ishmael

4. Isaac

5. The term used to describe the ritual of circumcision of an eight-day-old Jewish male

GENESIS [22-23]
THE BINDING OF ISAAC

Bible Review

FIND THE OUTSIDER*

Circle the letter before the statement or phrase that you think is incorrect or out of place.

1. Abraham   (a) obeyed God's command without question   (b) hid his plans from Isaac until the very last moment   (c) was praised and blessed by the Lord for showing his faith   (d) had inner doubts about fulfilling God's command   (e) did the actual work of preparing the sacrifice himself, rather than leaving it to his servants

2. Issac   (a) was deeply loved by Abraham   (b) suspected Abraham's plan from the start, but said and did nothing because of his love for his father   (c) helped Abraham prepare the altar   (d) was called Abraham's *only* son by the Lord and His angel   (e) traveled from the hills of Moriah to Beer-sheba

3. After Abraham proved his profound faith, God   (a) blessed him   (b) blessed his descendants   (c) promised never to put Abraham or his descendants to such a test again   (d) included all the peoples of the earth in His blessing   (e) predicted that Abraham would have a multitude of descendants

4. Sarah   (a) had nothing to do with the *akédah*   (b) was the only member of her immediate family who was not related to Ishmael   (c) died in a land far away from her birthplace   (d) was deeply mourned by Abraham   (e) died before Abraham as a punishment for laughing at the prediction that she would bear a son in her old age   (f) was buried in the land promised to Abraham and his descendants

33

5. Abraham's dealings with Ephron the Hittite revealed   (a) the hatred and state of war that existed between Abraham and the Canaanites   (b) the respect with which Abraham was thought of throughout the land   (c) that Abraham was a man of considerable economic worth   (d) that the Hittites were a generous people who placed value upon gestures of honor   (e) that Abraham believed in paying for whatever he received   (f) that Abraham could be a stubborn individual on occasion   (g) that burial of the dead was considered a ceremony of great importance in the ancient Near East

WHO, WHAT, OR WHERE?*

1. The place where Sarah died. _____

2. The animal who was sacrificed in place of Isaac. _____

3. The land where Abraham was commanded to travel in order to sacrifice Isaac. _____

4. The being who stopped Abraham from killing Isaac. _____

_____

5. The individual who provided Abraham with land in which to bury Sarah. _____

6. The cave that has been known through the ages as the burial place of Sarah and, later, of Abraham and other Hebrew patriarchs.

_____

Midrash Review

THE REASONS WHY

Complete the sentences below in terms of your understanding of the Midrash.

1. According to the Midrash, God commanded Abraham to sacrifice

Isaac as a burnt offering because _____

_____

_____

2. According to legend, the hill in Moriah was selected as the site of the sacrifice because _____

_____

_____

3. The Midrash explains that Abraham, rather than his servants, saddled his donkey because _____

_____

_____

A paper Simḥat Torah flag from Poland (nineteenth century) showing scenes from the story of the binding of Isaac.

4. According to rabbinic interpretation, Abraham was commanded to spare Isaac by an angel of the Lord, rather than by God Himself, because _____

_____

_____

5. According to ancient legend, Satan revealed to Isaac what lay in store for him because _____

_____

_____

but Satan's words were ignored because _____

_____

_____

LOOKING FOR UNDERSTANDING

1. What values are revealed by the following statements from the Midrash?

   a. "Of this the rabbis say: to destroy we need the authority of God Himself, but even the smallest angel can serve to show mercy." [5]

   b. "Why did God say 'please' to a mortal? Because He recognized how difficult His command was." [1]

   c. "When God commands, . . . one does not call a servant." [3]

d. "Not even the truth is accepted from the liar and the scorner." [4]

e. "That the world might know why I chose you from all others, . . . when they witnessed your loyalty and trust in Me." [1]

f. "I, the God of Righteousness, do not wish such offerings. . . . Human sacrifice is an abomination to Me." [1]

g. "As they [the two brothers] embraced, the Lord looked down and said, 'This place is holy. Here shall My glory rest.' " [2]

2. Discuss the various values that you find in the legend of the two brothers.

Summing Up

MAP STUDY: AN OLD-NEW LAND*

On the following page there is a map of modern Israel. The numbered black dots (which correspond to the numbered statements that follow) are locations that are discussed either in the biblical text or in the Midrash. The statements describe these locations, both in ancient and

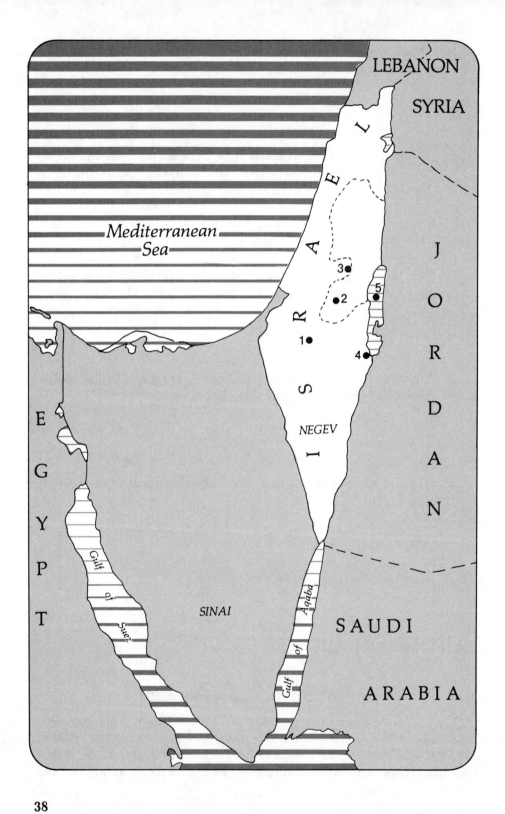

Mediterranean
Sea

LEBANON

SYRIA

ISRAEL

JORDAN

EGYPT

NEGEV

SINAI

Gulf of Suez

Gulf of Aqaba

SAUDI

ARABIA

38

modern terms. On the basis of each description, write in the name of the location referred to alongside its number on the map.

1. The city known in Israel today as the gateway to the Negev, where Abraham lived for many years, and to which he returned after the agonizing test of the akédah—the binding of Isaac.

2. The city where Sarah died and was buried, and a main point of bitter dispute between Arab and Jew in this century.

3. The hill, recognized today as the site of the holy temple built by Solomon, where Abraham was said to have put up the altar upon which he intended to sacrifice Isaac.

4. The Israeli city—today the site of a huge potash works—whose name has stood for evil, corruption, and destruction for thousands of years.

5. The famous body of water upon whose shores #4 is located, and whose Hebrew and English names have different meanings.

A CHARACTER SKETCH OF ABRAHAM: PART II

A great deal has happened since we last studied Abraham's (then called Abram) personality. What do the following statements, events, and Midrashic commentaries, from chapters 4 and 5, tell you about Abraham's character?

1. Abraham's laughter at being told that he and Sarah would together have a son.

_____

_____

_____

2. Abraham's hospitality toward the three strangers.

_____

_____

_____

3. Abraham's pleas to God to spare the citizens of Sodom and Gomorrah.

_____

_____

_____

4. Abraham's behavior toward his idol-worshiping guest, in terms of Abraham's anger, his acceptance of God's rebuke, and his ultimate apology to the old man. (See Chapter 4, Midrash [1])

_____

_____

_____

5. Abraham's obedience to God's command that he sacrifice Isaac.

_____

_____

_____

6. The discussions between Abraham and Ephron the Hittite about the purchase of a burial ground. (For example: How was Abraham regarded by his Canaanite neighbors? In what manner did Abraham deal with them?)

_____

_____

_____

GENESIS [24-25]

ISAAC AND REBEKAH

Bible Review

FROM WHAT YOU KNOW...

Point out the sources within the biblical text (by giving either a direct quotation, or your own brief summary) from which each of the following statements may be derived. At times, a statement may have several sources within this chapter. One reference is all that is necessary. (For example, Abraham had a strong and abiding faith in God. You might summarize: He traveled to an unknown land at the Lord's command; or, He was willing to sacrifice Isaac.)

1. Abraham was a man of considerable wealth.

2. Despite all the years that he had lived in the land, and despite the good relations that he enjoyed with his neighbors, Abraham still felt like a stranger among the Canaanites.

3. Isaac deeply loved and respected his mother, and grieved for her a long time.

4. Eliezer was greatly trusted and given much authority by Abraham.

5. Eliezer was very devoted and deeply committed to Abraham.

6. Rebekah's father and brother, Bethuel and Laban, recognized and respected God's power.

7. The members of Rebekah's family were concerned for her well-being, and they honored her wishes.

8. Abraham was not at all certain that he would live to see Isaac get married.

9. To Abraham, living in the land promised to him and his descendants by the Lord was a value of first importance.

10. Eliezer's choice of a wife for Isaac was based upon two considerations: who she was, and how she acted.

11. In addition to being kind and hospitable, Rebekah was a brave woman with a mind of her own.

12. Though he could not see the future in specific terms, Abraham's faith in God's will and His way was unshakable.

Midrash Review

WORD SCRAMBLE*

Unscramble the following words, each of which applies to Rebekah as she is described in the Midrash. Then, unscramble the thirteen circled letters to discover a human quality that has been deeply and constantly cherished by the Lord.

1. eytabu

2. sorgeenyti

3. sipomansco

4. ugaroce

5. lehera

LOOKING FOR UNDERSTANDING

The Midrash offers a number of insights into the needs and values that led to the choice of Rebekah as Isaac's wife. On the basis of what you have read, answer the following questions:

1. Why did Abraham insist that Isaac not marry a Canaanite?

   _____

   _____

   _____

2. Which of the following descriptions has not been applied to Rebekah? Circle the letter before the description(s) you choose.

   (a) wealthy   (b) beautiful   (c) compassionate

   (d) democratic   (e) athletic   (f) hospitable

   (g) unafraid to do what she felt was right despite the opinions of others

3. Why did Rebekah's offer to water his camels convince Eliezer that she was the right woman for Isaac?

   _____

   _____

   _____

4. In what sense was Isaac comforted by Rebekah?

   _____

   _____

   _____

5. What do Midrashim [4] and [5] show us about the place of women in Jewish tradition?

   _____

   _____

   _____

   _____

Summing Up

A LADDER OF VALUES

1. Values played a major role in Eliezer's encounter with Rebekah. He sought a woman who was not only Abraham's relative, but who also had certain personal qualities. Values play just as important a role in our lives today—helping us decide how we dress, where we live, who our friends are, what kind of a career we pursue, and how we conduct ourselves. Below are a series of values that people have traditionally cherished. Place them in what you think is the order of their importance to you and your circle of friends.

good looks　　　　high intelligence　　　　great wealth
compassion for other people　　　being well dressed
a strong cultural background　　　a sharp sense of humor
personal honesty　　　high professional status
athletic talent

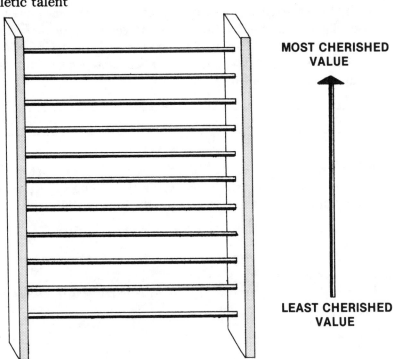

MOST CHERISHED
VALUE

LEAST CHERISHED
VALUE

2. Are there any values you would add to the list above? If so, where would you place these values on the ladder?

ELIEZER'S NOTEBOOK*

Abraham's life was filled with important events. And Eliezer, "the oldest servant of his house," was a witness to most of them. Imagine that a hard-working, and extremely lucky, archaeologist happened to discover Eliezer's notebook (which he would have kept on broken pieces of pottery) in which these various events were duly and accurately recorded. To which event does each of the following excerpts from Eliezer's notebook refer? (For this exercise you will have to consider the text and midrashim of chapters 3–6.)

1. Some called him a bad son, disrespectful and destructive. But he did what he did for the best of reasons: to make his father aware of the worthiness of the One God, and of the worthlessness of graven images.

   _____

   _____

2. Well, here we go again—pulling up roots for a second time, to settle in a distant land that we've never even seen. But Abram insists that he is obeying the command of his One God, and somehow his faith is contagious; I feel a sense of confidence in whatever the future will bring.

   _____

   _____

3. Whatever bitterness or bad blood may have existed before because of their servants' squabbles is certainly a thing of the past now. Abram put his life, and our lives, on the line for that nephew of his.

   _____

   _____

4. I am certainly happy for Abram; this is truly a blessed event for him. But I feel pity for Sarai.

   _____

   _____

5. Everything is so cloaked in mystery. My master refused to let me even saddle his donkey. All he would say is that he is going to the

land of Moriah. Now why would he want to go there?

_____

_____

6. Incredible! The changes that a person has to get used to. And after 99 years at that! I felt like saying "What's in a name?" but decided to keep my mouth shut.

_____

_____

7. I must confess, the ways of the One God are strange to me. I thought He would praise my master for the fact that he gave the old nonbeliever the boot; instead, He scolded Abraham.

_____

_____

8. This is a miracle that *has* to go down in the record books. I've never heard of anything like it before. It defies every law of nature. I am so happy for Sarah, happy that nothing "is impossible for the Lord."

_____

_____

9. It was the most horrifying sight that I ever saw in my life. All of that destruction. Every living thing wiped out.

_____

_____

10. My master's faith was truly well-founded. As beautiful in character as in looks—and a relative, too.

_____

_____

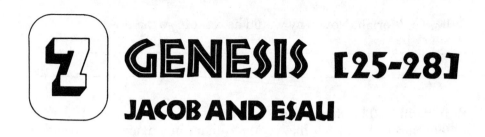

GENESIS [25-28]
JACOB AND ESAU

Bible Review

WHAT THE TORAH SAYS*

All of the choices following the statements below are possibilities for completing the sentences. Only one, however, is precise—in the sense that it can be specifically supported by the content of the text. Circle the letter before the precise passage to complete each sentence.

1. Rebekah ordered Jacob to go to the house of her brother Laban in Haran because   (a) she wanted Jacob to get to know her brother and his family   (b) she was concerned that Jacob would take a Hittite woman as a wife   (c) she wanted to spare Isaac from witnessing further fighting between the two brothers   (d) she feared that Esau would kill Jacob as soon as Isaac died   (e) she did not want Isaac to learn of her role in deceiving him

2. Isaac particularly loved his firstborn because   (a) Esau was a man of the outdoors   (b) Esau was physically stronger and more capable than Jacob   (c) he was fond of game meat   (d) Esau was the friendlier of the two   (e) Jacob was an intellectual, whose ways were strange to Isaac

3. From the story of the sale of Esau's birthright, we learn that   (a) Esau never placed high value upon his birthright   (b) an oath was taken seriously by both brothers   (c) Esau felt that everyday things were far more important than future promises such as birthrights and blessings   (d) Jacob was an expert bargainer   (e) Jacob was a superb cook

4. Jacob deceived Isaac and received his blessing because   (a) he and Esau never got along with one another   (b) he wanted

48

Isaac's blessing more than anything in the world   (c) he was angry because Isaac seemed to love Esau more than him   (d) he felt that the blessing really belonged to him because Esau sold him the birthright   (e) Rebekah insisted that he do so

5. Abimelech drove Isaac out of his land because   (a) Isaac had grown very rich and powerful   (b) Isaac and his family were disliked by their Philistine neighbors   (c) The Philistines were afraid that Isaac would cheat them in business dealings   (d) the Philistines were angry because Isaac looked down upon their gods   (e) the Philistines were used to dealing harshly with strangers—that is, non-Philistines

6. After learning of Jacob's deception, Isaac   (a) suspected that Rebekah had been involved   (b) worried about possible conflicts between the two brothers   (c) blamed himself for not seeing through Jacob's disguise   (d) promised Esau that one day he would no longer serve Jacob   (e) wondered whether it was a punishment for a sin that he had committed

TRUE OR FALSE?*

1. Isaac loved Esau more than Jacob, because Esau was his firstborn son. T [   ]   F [   ]

2. Rebekah's difficult pregnancy foretold a struggle not only between her unborn sons, but between their descendants, as well. T [   ]   F [   ]

3. Isaac's dealings with his Philistine neighbors took a turn for the worse because of his great wealth. T [   ]   F [   ]

4. Rebekah, like her mother-in-law before her, was unable to give birth for many years. T [   ]   F [   ]

5. Rebekah favored Jacob because Isaac favored Esau. T [   ]   F [   ]

6. When the Lord made His covenant with Abraham, Isaac, and Jacob, there was never any mention of riches. T [   ]   F [   ]

7. One reason that Jacob did not want to dress up as Esau was that he feared he would be discovered. T [   ]   F [   ]

8. Once Isaac's blessing was given, it could not be taken back, even though Isaac discovered that Jacob had deceived him. T [ ] F [ ]

9. Water was often the cause of bitter argument between Isaac and his neighbors. T [ ] F [ ]

10. Abimelech made peace with Isaac because he saw that the land was big enough for both of them. T [ ] F [ ]

11. Isaac, like Abraham before him, was opposed to intermarriage with the surrounding Canaanites. T [ ] F [ ]

12. After he discovered Jacob's trickery, Isaac lost all interest in his younger son's future. T [ ] F [ ]

Midrash Review

HOW MIDRASH EXPLAINS

This chapter contains many conflicts, plots, and shows of emotion. Using the Midrash as your source, explain the following:

1. Why did Rebekah insist that Jacob take Isaac's blessing in place of Esau?

_____

_____

_____

2. Why, in the opinion of the rabbis, did Isaac favor Esau over Jacob?

_____

_____

_____

3. Why did Esau place so little value upon his birthright that he was

willing to trade it for a serving of lentil pottage?

_____

_____

_____

4. Why did Isaac ask Jacob to "Come near. . .that I may feel you, to see whether you are really my son Esau, or not"?

_____

_____

_____

5. Why did Esau's friends mock and laugh at Jacob?

_____

_____

_____

6. Why did Jacob at first not wish to give Esau the plate of lentils and eggs for which he asked?

_____

_____

_____

LOOKING FOR UNDERSTANDING

Discuss the ideas, good or bad, that you find in the following sentences from the Midrash. At times a single statement may contain several ideas; and ideas within the same excerpt may not agree with one another.

1. "Their models have been heroes of the spirit; prophets and scholars." Midrash [3]

2. "Each brother wished to be born first, so as to win the birthright.

When Esau threatened to kill their mother, Jacob let him go first, but held on to his heel." Midrash [1]

3. "Life too is like a wheel: for every death there is a birth; life ends, and life begins." Midrash [5]

4. "Then Rebekah said, '. . . It is Esau's mother who says he does not deserve the blessing, for he spurns God and takes foreign wives. I command you to take his place!' " Midrash [7]

5. "Look at the fool! I ate his lentils, drank his wine, and do you know what I gave him for these good things? My birthright!" Midrash [6]

Summing Up

PERMANENTLY SET APART

In Chapter 6, Rebekah was singled out because she was different, set apart in her actions and outlook on life, from her family and friends. The Jewish people have been socially and spiritually different from their neighbors since the days of Abraham, who—as the Midrash tells us—opposed majority opinion by scorning and smashing idols, and by worshiping the One God. Both Abraham and Isaac would not allow their sons to intermarry with the local peoples, and Jacob was not a hunter or a warrior, as was the fashion then, but a prophet and a scholar. Throughout the Bible, the Children of Israel are taught not to adopt the pagan ways of their neighbors, not to be a "nation like other nations," but to preserve their special traditions and values. And during the past 2,000 years, the greatest danger from within Jewish life has been assimilation—adopting the customs and culture of the surrounding society so completely that Jewish identity is lost in the process. Thus, being set apart, at least in certain ways, has proved to be central to the survival of Judaism and Jewish life.

In the space below, tell how you and other Jews you know are set apart from your non-Jewish neighbors. In what sense does being Jewish mean being different?

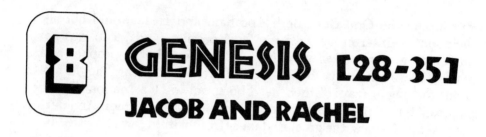

GENESIS [28-35]
JACOB AND RACHEL

Bible Review

JACOB'S MAP*

Below is an imaginary discovery that any archaeologist would regard as priceless: the map upon which Jacob recorded his journeys, from the moment that he fled his father's house in fear of Esau, until his return some 20 years later. Each location that he refers to is pinpointed by a letter on the map. Next to the appropriate letter, fill in the name of the location described.

A. "The city, named by my father for the good fortune he found there, from which my travels began."

B. "Where I dreamt of the heavenly ladder."

C. "The home of my father-in-law, where I married and began to raise my family."

D. "Where I wrestled all night with the Lord, and where Esau and I were reunited."

E. "Where I buried my wife, Rachael."

F. "Where I saw my father again after many years."

IF IT HAPPENED TODAY*

If everything in this chapter had happened today, in the twentieth century, the events would have been much the same, but people would have used modern ways of speaking to one another. From the modern statements below; see if you can tell what biblical character might have

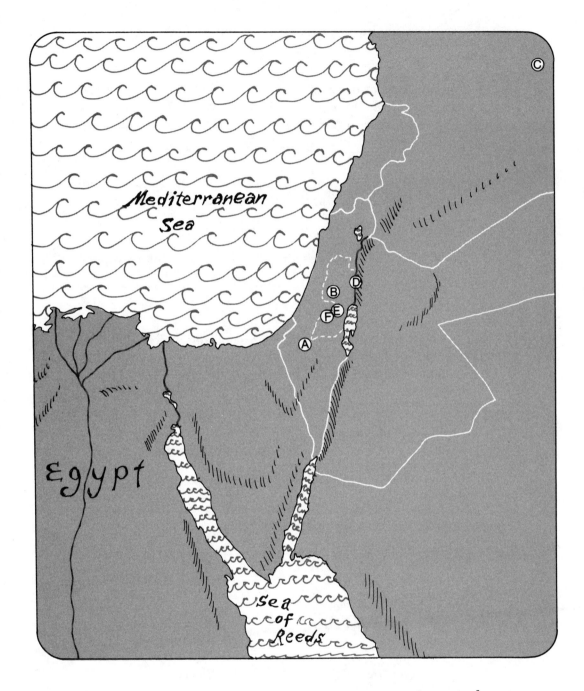

been speaking. Remember: the same character may have made more than one statement.

1. "No, I've never laid eyes on him before. But we are related, and he

is a hard worker, and my home is his home for as long as he likes." _____

2. "So this is the upshot of all tricks that we pulled off. Here I am, a runaway, a fugitive. Who knows when, or even if, I'll ever see my family again. What's that old saying about Mother knowing best? I'm not so sure." _____

3. "Maybe I'm nearsighted, but I'm not blind. I can read the hand-writing on the wall, just as I can read what's in your heart— and it's not love for me!" _____

4. "I said to him, 'Let bygones of 20 years ago or more remain bygones. Besides, blood's thicker than water.' " _____

_____

5. "You say that I cheated you? That's a good one. When it comes to cheating, you are a professor of trickery. Or have you for-gotten why you came to my house in the first place?"

_____

6. "That was a night to remember! The toughest fight of my life! How did I survive? Only God knows. To me it remains a mystery. And a miracle." _____

7. "Knowing that my sons have patched up their differences and are behaving like brothers, instead of bitter enemies, is blessing enough for me. Now, I can die in peace." _____

Midrash Review

LOOKING FOR UNDERSTANDING

In your own words, identify the major ideas that you find in the following statements from the Midrash.

1. "On his journey he came to a resting place for travelers, set up by

thoughtful people because there was no inn." Midrash [2]

2. "When he awoke, he said, 'I know now that God is found not only in sanctuaries, but wherever people do good for their fellow man.' " Midrash [2]

3. "Jacob prayed that the twelve tribes be ever as one, united as brothers and in serving the Lord." Midrash [5]

4. "It is as though man's deeds give rise to the angels." Midrash [3]

5. "As long as heaven and earth exist, the Jews shall be the world's conscience, bringing God's light to mankind." Midrash [4]

6. "A righteous man is the splendor, beauty and glory of a town; when he leaves, these depart with him." Midrash [1]

Summing Up

PRESENT AND PAST

Present and past are closely related in Jewish life. We are part of an evergrowing history and tradition. In the left column are a group of Jewish values as they might be stated today. Fill in the blank spaces opposite each statement, with statements from the text or Midrash that you think best capture the spirit of the particular value. (A value may be expressed in more than one way, and in a number of passages; you make what, in your opinion, is the best choice.)

1. The Hebrew word for helping the poor is not "charity," but *tzedakah,* "righteousness."

   _____
   _____
   _____

2. The basic unit in Jewish life is the *kehillah*—a strong, united Jewish community— whose members do their best to live by the letter and spirit of the *mitzvot,* Judaism's laws!

   _____
   _____
   _____
   _____
   _____

3. Judaism traditionally gives priority to the moral, rather than the merely ritual, commandments. How you treat fellow human beings is more important to God than the ceremonies by which you worship Him.

   _____
   _____
   _____
   _____
   _____

4. One of Judaism's cornerstones is the idea of the unity of the Jewish people, wherever they happen to be. To repeat, *Kol Yisrael Arevim Zeh Ba-Zeh,* "All of Israel, every Jew, is responsible for one another."

   _____
   _____
   _____
   _____
   _____

5. A second cornerstone is the central importance of Eretz Israel, the Land of Israel, to Jewish life.

_____

_____

_____

_____

NAMES AND THEIR MEANINGS*

Match each Hebrew name in the left column (these come from Chapters 7 and 8) to the statement in the right column that comes closest to its meaning.

1. Beer-sheba   _____ House of God

2. Esau   _____ One who wrestles with the Lord

3. Jacob   _____ He has judged

4. Beth-el   _____ "Behold, a son!"

5. Benjamin   _____ The well of good fortune

6. Reuben   _____ "May He add. . ."

7. Peniel   _____ One who holds on by the heel

8. Israel   _____ The son of the right hand

9. Dan   _____ Hairy one

10. Joseph   _____ Face of God

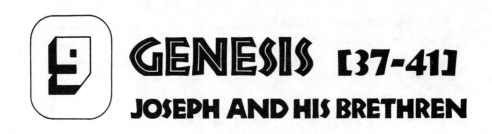

GENESIS [37-41]
JOSEPH AND HIS BRETHREN

Bible Review

FILL IN THE BLANKS*

Write the words below in the correct blank spaces to complete the story that follows.

annoy   serve   instincts   resented   fuel

hostility   favored   Egypt   squealer

Joseph was bitterly _____ by his brothers, not only because Jacob clearly _____ him over them but because he, himself, added _____ to the fire. To begin with, he was something of a _____, bringing bad reports of his brothers to their father. In addition, he had dreams, in which he foretold that his brothers would one day _____ him. These predictions even managed to _____ his father, who sharply rebuked him for his arrogance. And so, when he went to see his brothers who were tending their flocks far from home, their _____ toward him got the better of their good _____. They threw Joseph into a pit, and finally sold him to a group of Ishmaelites who brought him to _____.

WHO SAID WHAT?*

Joseph was a character who sparked powerful reactions in others. Some loved him, and held him in great esteem; others hated him so deeply that they went to great physical and moral lengths to do him harm (conspiring, lying, or putting their own good names on the line)—but love him or hate him, everyone talked about him. On the basis of your knowledge of the text, which of the characters listed below might have made the following statements about Joseph? (You may use a name more than once, and some names you may not even need.)

Pharaoh   Potiphar   Judah   Jacob

Potiphar's wife   Pharaoh's cupbearer

Pharaoh's baker   Reuben   Dinah

1. I was so happy and relieved over my good fortune that I promptly put him out of my mind. He was a stranger, but even so, a promise is a promise, and I broke mine to him. _____

2. I love him as much as ever, but his dreams are getting on my nerves. He is getting just a bit too big for his britches. _____

3. Who does he think he is? He is a stranger, a servant—and yet he dares to disobey me. I'll pay him back for this humiliation!

_____

4. No! I didn't like him, I admit that. But if it were not for me, he would be dead now. Maybe he was sold into slavery because of me, but he's alive because of me, as well!

_____

5. Why do I give so much power and glory to a stranger? Because I've got to adopt the policy that is best for the country. It is my duty!

_____

6. Oh no! I came to him all full of faith and hope! And what does he tell me? That my days are numbered! _____

7. I know playing favorites is wrong, but I couldn't help myself. It was a matter of feeling, pure and simple! And now, I'll be in mourning the rest of my life._____

8. After all I did for him, look at what he did to me! He's lucky to be alive, let me tell you._____

Midrash Review

*FIND THE OUTSIDER**

In each of the following statements, circle the letter before the phrase that does not belong.

1. The story of the coat of many colors teaches us that   (a) Jacob's love for Joseph moved him to act unwisely   (b) Jacob only loved the children of Rachel   (c) small acts can bring about large, and long-range, results   (d) a parent should not favor one child over another

2. The story of the cupbearer and the baker teaches us that (a) Pharaoh had the power of life and death over his servants (b) laziness or negligence on the part of servants was not permitted in the Pharaoh's court   (c) Pharaoh's advisers tried to be just and fair in their judgments   (d) Pharaoh liked the cupbearer more than he did the baker   (e) the cupbearer may have been as lax in performing his duties as was the baker, but there was no way of proving it

3. In the story of Joseph and Potiphar,   (a) Joseph showed Potiphar the nature and extent of God's power   (b) Potiphar was suspicious at first of Joseph's religious practices   (c) the household servants were very jealous of Joseph's rise to power and plotted against him   (d) Joseph showed that he was not above imitating the ways of the Egyptians at the expense of his own identity and heritage   (e) we see that God watched over Joseph in Egypt

4. The stories of how Joseph was taken to Egypt show that   (a) Joseph's brothers were not sure of what to do with him   (b) Reuben was the first to realize what a terrible thing had been done   (c) the brothers were sorry for their actions and tried to bring Joseph back   (d) without Judah's advice, the brothers might have gone ahead and killed Joseph   (e) once Joseph disappeared, his brothers sadly realized how much they loved him   (f) the brothers, fearing their father's reaction, tried to cover up their deed with a lie.

5. Pharaoh gave Joseph a position of immense power and prestige

because   (a) he felt that only a foreigner would be able to command the respect of the Egyptian people   (b) he accepted Joseph's interpretation of his dreams   (c) he was impressed by Joseph's qualities   (d) he was disappointed in the interpretations and advice given by his own people   (e) his first concern was getting the job done, and he believed that Joseph was the best person to do it

THE REASONS WHY

In your own words, summarize the explanations given by the Midrash for the following.

1. Joseph was pursued by Potiphar's wife because _____

_____

Probably the tomb of some medieval Islamic dignitary, but since the Bible states that Rachel died nearby, the legend arose amongst Moslems and Jews that this is her tomb.

2. Pharaoh's cupbearer was forgiven while his baker was hanged because_____

_____

3. The generations of Jacob begin with Joseph rather than with Jacob's other sons because _____

_____

4. Joseph was pulled out of the pit by his brothers because _____

_____

5. Joseph's brothers made up the story of his being devoured by a wild beast because _____

_____

6. Pharaoh told his dreams far more fully to Joseph than he did to his magicians because _____

_____

7. Pharaoh appointed Joseph, over his own soothsayers and officers, to be viceroy of Egypt because _____

_____

Summing Up

A STRATEGY FOR SURVIVAL

The passage in Midrash [7] ("Soon he was enjoying his power and comfort. He began to curl his hair and to dress elegantly after the Egyptian fashion.") teaches us that assimilation is a constant threat to Jewish life. Like Joseph, who "forgot about his . . . father," Jews today are in danger of forgetting their history, their values, their heritage, and their commitments. Imagine that you are several years older and married, with two or three young children. In the space below, discuss some of the ways in which you would work to raise your children as strong, committed Jews, capable of resisting the forces of assimilation.

WHAT MADE THEM DO IT?*

Match the happenings in the right column with their causes in the left column.

1. Concern for his
   country's well-being

_____ The farfetched interpretations of Pharaoh's dreams by his Egyptian advisers

2. Fear of discovery

_____ Joseph's brothers' act of casting him in the pit, with the intention to kill him

3. Desire for power

_____ The pardoning of Pharaoh's cupbearer

4. Jealousy and hatred

_____ Pharaoh's appointment of Joseph as Egyptian viceroy

5. The desire to do justice

_____ The brothers' presentation of Joseph's bloodied coat to Jacob

10 GENESIS [42-45]
JOSEPH IN EGYPT

Bible Review

NEWS HEADLINE*

Imagine that the events in this chapter were recorded in a modern daily newspaper (*The Canaan Chronicle*, or *The Egyptian Evening News*, for example). To which events do you think the following updated news headlines refer?

1. ALLEGED CANAANITE SPY RING UNCOVERED BY GOVERNER!

   _____

   _____

2. FATHER REFUSES TO ACT TO RELEASE IMPRISONED SON!

   _____

   _____

3. BROTHERS WORRY ABOUT SURPRISE BONANZA! FEAR NEW ACCUSATIONS AND PUNISHMENT!

   _____

   _____

4. FAMILY HEAD FINALLY GIVES IN; "CHOICE BETWEEN POSSIBLE DANGER AND CERTAIN DEATH!" HE DECLARES

   _____

   _____

5. "TAKE ME!" INSISTS YOUNG FELON'S OLDER BROTHER

_____

_____

6. "BYGONES ARE BYGONES" THEME OF FAMILY REUNION!

_____

_____

CREATING HEADLINES

This is an exercise in imagination—your own. Try creating headlines to describe the following events. (Make them dramatic and modern.)

1. The reunion between Joseph and his brothers when Joseph revealed his true identity

_____

2. Judah's vow to Jacob concerning Benjamin's safety

_____

3. The seizure and imprisonment of Simeon in Egypt

_____

4. And, in the space below, you choose an event from the chapter which captures your creative fancy for headline-making.

_____

TRUE OR FALSE*

1. The brothers went down to Egypt a second time in order to free Simeon. T [   ] F [   ]

2. Joseph deliberately lied when he accused his brothers of being spies. T [   ] F [   ]

3. The famine predicted by Joseph to Pharaoh (Chapter 9) struck not only Egypt, but other countries in the area, as well. T [   ] F [   ]

4. Joseph, though remembered and mourned by his father, was all but forgotten by his brothers. T [   ] F [   ]

5. The brothers were delighted to open their sacks and find not only the grain that they had purchased, but the money that they had paid, as well.   T [   ]   F [   ]

6. The brothers were very jealous that the portion given to Benjamin by Joseph was five times as great as any of theirs.   T [   ]   F [   ]

7. When Joseph's goblet was discovered in Benjamin's sack, the brothers gave him up without an argument.   T [   ]   F [   ]

8. Joseph did not blame his brothers for sending him to Egypt because he believed that they were acting as instruments of God's will.   T [   ]   F [   ]

9. Joseph did not recognize his brothers until they told him about their family and where they came from.   T [   ]   F [   ]

10. The brothers believed that their troubles in Egypt were a punishment for what they had done to Joseph.   T [   ]   F [   ]

Midrash Review

LOOKING FOR UNDERSTANDING

Using the Midrash as your source, answer the following questions:

1. What arguments did Judah use so that Jacob would send Benjamin to Egypt?

_____

_____

2. Why did Joseph reveal his identity just when Judah pleaded to take Benjamin's punishment himself?

_____

_____

3. Why did Pharaoh not wish to sell grain at first?

_____

_____

4. Who acted as interpreter between Joseph and his brothers, and what does this tell us about Joseph's values?

_____

_____

_____

5. Why did Joseph not arrange an immediate reunion with his aged and grieving father when he became a man of power in Egypt?

_____

_____

_____

6. Why did Joseph wish to conceal his identity from his brothers?

_____

_____

_____

Summing Up

FROM WHAT YOU READ

Support the following statements with quotations from either the text or the Midrash. (In many cases, there may be several possible quotations; any one will do.)

1. Joseph's brothers felt guilt and regret at having sold him into slavery.

_____

_____

_____

2. Joseph believed that his coming to Egypt was the will of God.

_____

_____

_____

3. Judah showed himself to be a man of integrity, courage, and wisdom.

_____

_____

_____

4. Jacob had never ceased grieving for his lost son, Joseph.

_____

_____

_____

5. Joseph continued to love his brothers, despite what they had done to him.

_____

_____

_____

6. Joseph was determined to preserve his heritage and identity, regardless of the power and position that he enjoyed in Egypt.

_____

_____

_____

7. Jacob's sons changed for the better in the years since they sold Joseph into slavery.

_____

_____

_____

WHY WE DO WHAT WE DO

The Bible is concerned not only with what we do, but with why we do things. People are very complex; they are always changing, but they usually have reasons for acting the way that they act. In the space beneath each action given in this exercise, try to fill in the reason or reasons that you think the person acting might have had. You can use the text and the Midrash as resources.

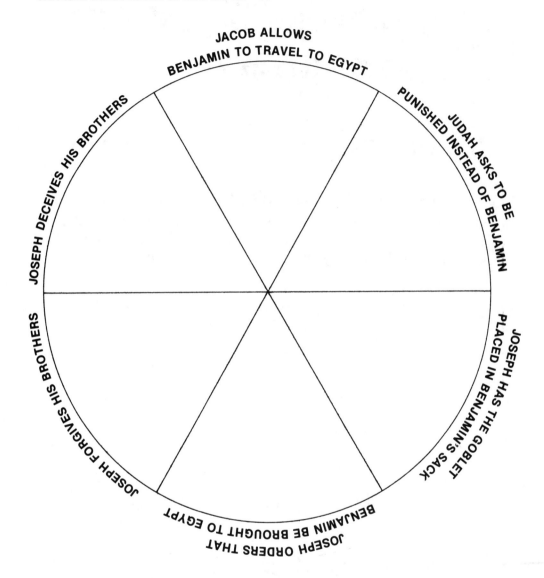

11 GENESIS [45-50]
ISRAEL IN EGYPT

Bible Review

LEAVES FROM A REPORTER'S NOTEBOOK*

A reporter for our imaginary newspaper has been studying the lives of the patriarchs and has made notes in an imaginative way—on "leaves"! Use the notes to fill in the newspaper story as it later appeared.

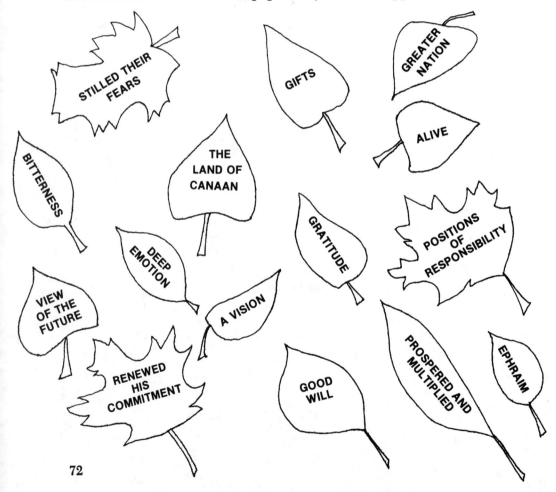

When Jacob learned that Joseph was _____,
his shock and disbelief gave way to _____
when he saw the wagons full of _____ that
his son had sent in greeting. He knew that he would never again see
_____, but the Lord had comforted him
with _____ in which He reaffirmed His
promise.

The reunion between Jacob and Joseph was marked by
_____. Pharaoh showed his
_____ again and again, offering Joseph's
family fertile land upon which to settle, as well as _____
_____ overseeing his herds. He listened to
Jacob's story of his life, and finally received _____
from the aged patriarch. And then, as God had promised, Jacob's family
_____ in the land of Goshen.

As his death drew near, Jacob _____ to
the land of his ancestors, and to his ties with the past. He
_____ Joseph by blessing Ephraim and
Manasseh _____; however, Jacob explained
to his son that it was not old age or bad eyesight that made him do this,
but a _____ in which the descendants of
_____ would be the _____.

After Jacob's burial, Joseph comforted his brothers and
_____ by declaring that he felt no
_____ and would seek no
_____. He further told them that the Lord
would remember them and the Children of Israel and would one day
return to the Promised Land.

WHAT THE TORAH SAYS*

All of the items in the lettered statements below may be correct. Circle the letter before the one item that *exactly* matches the content of the text.

1. Among the things that Jacob discussed with Joseph when he was about to die was

   a. The education of Joseph's children.
   b. Joseph's moral conduct as viceroy of Egypt.
   c. Joseph's relations with his brothers after Jacob's death.
   d. Memories of Esau, Laban, Isaac, and Abraham.
   e. The location of Jacob's final resting place.
   f. Jacob's regret that he would never again see the land of Canaan.

2. When his brothers left Egypt for Canaan to fetch their father and his household, Joseph asked

   a. That they visit his mother's grave on the road to Bethlehem.
   b. That they take very good care of Benjamin.
   c. That they not fight with one another on the way to their homeland.
   d. That they gently break the news of Joseph's being alive to Jacob, in order not to shock him.
   e. That they tell Jacob of Joseph's rise to power in Egypt.

3. Upon hearing of Joseph's reunion with his brothers, Pharaoh

   a. Was surprised that they once hated Joseph so fiercely.
   b. Discovered that Joseph's ties with his family, his heritage, and his homeland were very strong.
   c. Marveled at Joseph's ability to forgive and forget.
   d. Promised Joseph that his family would be protected and provided for in Egypt.
   e. Was eager to meet Joseph's father.

4. After Jacob's death, Joseph's brothers

   a. Mourned their father from the depths of their hearts.
   b. Worried that, with Jacob gone, Joseph might now take revenge.
   c. Divided Jacob's wealth and worldly goods among themselves.
   d. Vowed never to abandon Jacob's beliefs and values.
   e. Competed with one another to find favor in Joseph's eyes.

5. Upon meeting Pharaoh, Jacob

    a. Thanked the ruler for giving refuge to him and his family.

    b. Told him about his grandfather Abraham's belief in the One God.

    c. Spoke of how much he loved Joseph, and how proud he was of him.

    d. Described the famine that had struck his homeland.

    e. Blessed the Egyptian ruler.

6. Jacob's blessing of Ephraim and Manasseh proved that

    a. Old men are often confused upon their deathbeds.

    b. Jacob was still willing to play favorites, as he did with Joseph many years earlier.

    c. Jacob believed he could predict the future.

    d. Jacob did not want to be told what to do by Joseph, despite his son's great power.

7. At the time of his death, Joseph

    a. Promised his brothers that they would continue to live in peace, prosperity, and security.

    b. Embraced Benjamin with great affection.

    c. Blessed his children, grandchildren, and great-grandchildren.

    d. Was upset that his life had been so much shorter than those of Abraham, Isaac, and Jacob.

    e. Promised his brothers that the Sons of Israel would be remembered by God, and brought back to the land of Canaan.

Midrash Review

A RESEARCH PROJECT

Using the Midrash as your reference, sum up Jacob's attitudes on the following subjects—and in each case, select a brief quotation from the Midrash to support what you say.

1. Jacob's feelings toward Canaan, the Holy Land

    a. (Your summary) _____

    _____

b. (Midrash quotation) _____

_____

(Midrash number [   ])

2. Jacob's attitude toward wealth, power, and position

a. (Your summary) _____

_____

b. (Midrash quotation) _____

_____

(Midrash [   ])

3. Jacob's opinion of Egyptian religious practices

a. (Your summary) _____

_____

b. (Midrash quotation) _____

_____

(Midrash [   ])

4. Jacob's relations with his Canaanite neighbors

a. (Your summary) _____

_____

b. (Midrash quotation) _____

_____

(Midrash [   ])

5. Jacob's definition of a worthy human being

a. (Your summary) _____

_____

b. (Midrash quotation) _____

_____

(Midrash [   ])

6. Jacob's ties with his dead father and grandfather

    a. (Your summary) _____

         _____

    b. (Midrash quotation) _____

         _____

                                       (Midrash [   ])

7. Jacob's attitudes toward assimilation

    a. (Your summary) _____

         _____

    b. (Midrash quotation) _____

         _____

                                       (Midrash [   ])

Summing Up

EXPLORING VALUES

In the space below, write down one value found in the Midrash, and explain how it may be applied to our life today.

Value_____

Explanation:

SYMPTOMS AND CAUSES

Midrash [4] speaks of Jacob's deep-down hatred and fear of assimilation—he did not want his children to imitate the customs, values, and life-style of the Egyptians. The pieces below stand for a Jewish community torn apart by assimilation. Inside these pieces, note what you think are the main reasons these things happen.

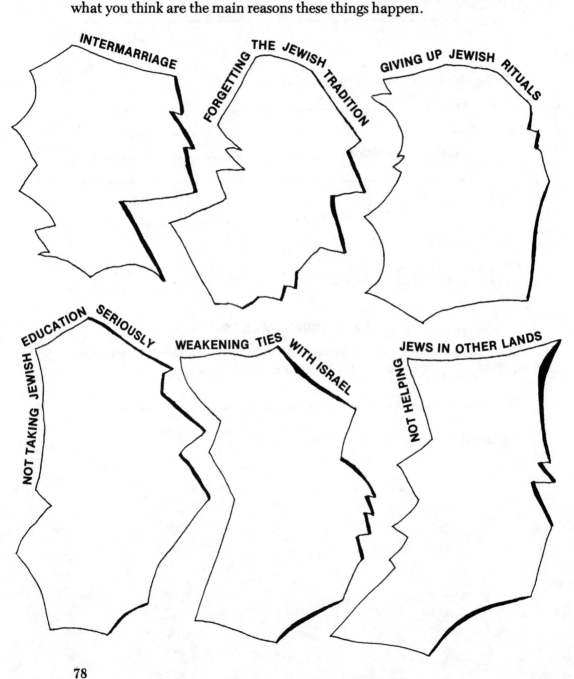

EXODUS [1-4]
THE OPPRESSION OF THE ISRAELITES

Bible Review

A ROUND ROBIN REVIEW*

Here's a chance to see how much of this chapter you remember.

1. Who, or What, Am I?

   a. The name of Moses' father-in-law _____

   b. His nationality and occupation _____

   c. The occupation of the people who disobeyed Pharaoh's order to

   kill all newborn Hebrew boys _____

   d. The two store-cities built by the Children of Israel for their

   Egyptian taskmasters _____

   e. The name of Moses' wife _____

   f. The location of the burning bush _____

   g. The name of Moses' brother _____

   h. The Israelite tribe of which Moses was a member

   _____

2. True or False?

   a. Although Moses' father-in-law was not a Hebrew, he understood why Moses had to return to his people in Egypt. T [   ] F [   ]

   b. Moses did not want to undertake the mission that God had assigned him. T [   ] F [   ]

c. If the daughter of Pharaoh had guessed that the infant she found in the basket was a Hebrew, she never would have brought the baby home. T [   ]   F [   ]

d. Moses left for Midian because he could no longer bear to see his people living in bondage. T [   ]   F [   ]

e. The Pharaohs of Egypt in the generations following Joseph's death grew to fear and suspect the Hebrew strangers in their midst. T [   ]   F [   ]

f. Moses was unsure that he could persuade the Pharaoh to free the Children of Israel. T [   ]   F [   ]

g. Moses did not believe in the Lord's power until he saw his rod turn into a serpent. T [   ]   F [   ]

h. God promised Moses that he would not be alone in his mission, that he would be aided by others. T [   ]   F [   ]

3. Effects and Causes

a. The infant, Moses, was placed in a basket among the reeds because _____

_____

b. Pharaoh condemned newborn Hebrew boys to death because

_____

_____

c. The Hebrew midwives disobeyed Pharaoh's command because

_____

d. Moses killed an Egyptian because _____

_____

e. The Lord grew angry with Moses because _____

_____

f. Aaron was commanded to meet Moses in the wilderness because

_____

4. Between the Lines

Match the characters in the left column with the statements that they might have made to one another in the right column.

a. Moses to Jethro ____ "I don't know who Joseph was, and I couldn't care less. Maybe he was a big hero in the days of old, but his descendants are a big worry to me today. Aliens, possible revolutionaries—I say put them to work. Let them repay our hospitality with some good, hard labor!"

b. A Hebrew midwife to an Egyptian official ____ "Maybe I shouldn't have opened my mouth. After all, the guy he killed was our enemy. But I just couldn't stand his preaching at me, so I told him off."

c. Moses to the Lord ____ "Look, I understand your wanting to dig up your roots. But it's a dangerous business. Particularly in these times. I've told you all I know. To me, you're my son— now and forever. I don't care where you came from, or what your family tree is."

d. One of the quarreling Hebrew slaves to his wife ____ "Okay, he is the big man, and these are his orders. But there is a higher power to whom I have to answer as well. And I can't see that higher power's approving of my murdering little babies!"

e. Pharaoh's daughter   _____ "I know you've given me a roof
    to Moses   over my head, work to do, a wife,
                                and a chance to rebuild my life.
                                But I've got to go home, to see my
                                people again. Please try to un-
                                derstand!"

f. Pharaoh to a   _____ "Why me? Just answer that one
    member of his court   simple question. Why of all the
                                descendants of Abraham, Isaac,
                                and Jacob have You chosen me?"

5. Find the Outsider
   (Circle the number of the choice that does not belong.)

   a. The reasons behind Pharaoh's harsh treatment of the Children
       of Israel were   (1) suspicion of strangers   (2) fear of their
       growing strength   (3) hatred of the One God they wor-
       shiped   (4) ignorance of his country's history   (5) worry
       over their loyalty to Egypt in a crisis

   b. Pharaoh's daughter adopted Moses as a son because   (1) she
       grew to love him   (2) she took pity on him   (3) she
       wanted a child to raise as her own   (4) this was her way of
       spiting and defying her father

   c. Among the reasons that Moses met and married Zipporah were
       (1) a desire for the special honor bestowed upon those who wed
       a Midianite maid   (2) her father Jethro's giving hospitality to
       Moses   (3) Moses' being forced to flee Egypt or be killed by
       the Pharaoh   (4) Moses' standing up to the Midianite
       shepherds, and protecting Jethro's daughters.

   d. Moses' reactions to God's command to "bring forth. . . the
       Children of Israel out of Egypt" included   (1) modesty and
       humility (2) his feeling that he could not succeed (3) a de-
       sire that the Lord choose someone else for this mission (4) fear
       of what might come to pass in the future   (5) disbelief in the
       presence and power of the Lord

Midrash Review

LOOKING FOR UNDERSTANDING

Using the Midrash as your main source, try answering the following questions:

1. Why did the Egyptians hate the Children of Israel for adopting their ways and worshiping their gods? After all, isn't imitation supposed to be a form of flattery?

_____

_____

_____

_____

_____

2. It's easy to understand why the Egyptians wanted to get as much work out of their Hebrew slaves as possible, but why did they spend so much time and energy dreaming up ways of humiliating them?

_____

_____

_____

_____

_____

3. Among the reasons given for the Israelites' not giving up hope were that "they never changed their names; they never changed their language." Why, and how, did these factors strengthen the spirit of the Hebrews?

_____

_____

_____

_____

_____

4. Many of the wives of the Hebrew slaves were models of the classic Jewish ideal of *Eishet Hayil*, a woman of valor. Why? How would valor be defined in this instance?

_____

_____

_____

_____

5. The Hebrew midwives of the period guarded the value of *Kol Yisrael Arevim Zeh Ba-Zeh* —that is, a sense of mutual responsibility among Jews, and a sense of involvement with, and commitment to, the Jewish community at large. How did they express this?

_____

_____

_____

_____

6. One might say that Moses was raised (if not born) with a silver spoon in his mouth. He grew up with every advantage. Why did he choose to throw all of this away by going to the aid of the Hebrew slaves, "bending his back beneath the huge stones they were struggling to put into place"? Midrash [6] _____

_____

_____

_____

_____

7. What does the burning bush stand for when we think of the experience of the Jewish people?

_____

_____

_____

_____

8. Why does the Midrash say, "And God said, 'Yes, even before you fulfill My command, ask Jethro's leave' "? Midrash [10]

_____

_____

_____

_____

Summing Up

A PROFILE OF MOSES

What can you tell about Moses' personality and character from the following quotations from the text and the Midrash?

1. "He. . . saw that two Hebrews were fighting. He said to the wrongdoer, 'Why do you strike your fellow?' "

_____

_____

_____

2. "Moses. . . said to God, 'First I must return to Midian to ask my father-in-law's permission to leave.' " Midrash [10]

_____

_____

_____

3. "And Moses said, 'O Lord, I pray Thee, send anyone but me.' "

_____

_____

_____

4. "Dismounting, Moses went to their aid, bending his back beneath the huge stones. . . . When he walked among them. . . his eyes were filled with tears." Midrash [6]

_____

_____

_____

5. "And Moses said, 'Who am I, that I should go to Pharaoh and that I should bring the Children of Israel out of Egypt?' "

_____

_____

_____

MAP STUDY*

Below is a map of modern Egypt and the surrounding areas. The numbers on this map show ancient locations that are referred to in the biblical text (both in this and previous chapters), and that are described next to corresponding numbers in the statements that follow. Fill in the

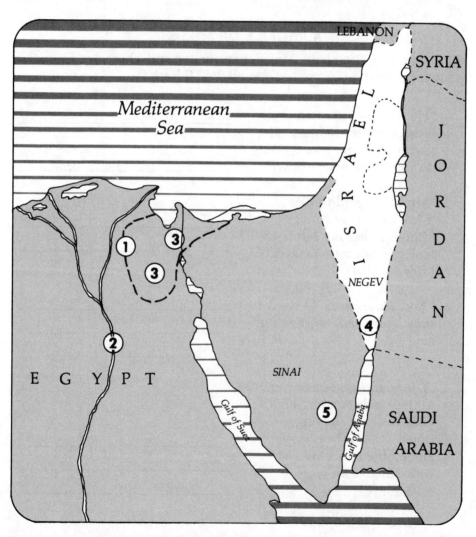

names of these ancient locations alongside their numbers on the map. (Large stretches of ancient territory are traced on the map with broken lines. The appropriate number is attached to one of the lines.)

1. The area of land given to Jacob and his family by the Pharaoh when they first arrived in Egypt

2. The site where the papyrus basket containing the infant, Moses, might have been found by Pharaoh's daughter

3. The two store-cities built by the Children of Israel for their Egyptian task masters

4. The land in which Moses found refuge and created a life for himself after fleeing from Egypt

5. The place where Moses saw the burning bush

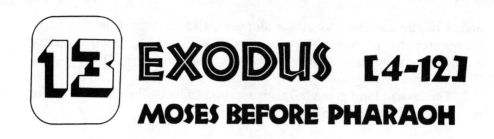

13 EXODUS [4-12]
MOSES BEFORE PHARAOH

Bible Review

A MEDIA MIX*

The Ten Plagues, visited upon Egypt because of the Pharaoh's greed, cruelty, and stubbornness, were very dramatic events—undoubtedly much discussed and agonized over by the Egyptians of the day. Imagine that the modern mass media—news headlines, editorials, and television coverage, for example—were in operation then. To which of the plagues would the following media descriptions refer?

1. THE INQUIRING REPORTER'S QUESTION OF THE DAY: "WHERE WERE YOU WHEN THE LIGHTS WENT OUT?"

_____

2. TV INTERVIEWER TO EGYPTIAN SCHOOL CHILDREN: "WERE YOU FRIGHTENED?"
Child #1: "The noise scared me a little."
Child #2: "I didn't mind the big booms, but the lights scared me. It was like the whole sky was on fire. . ."

_____

3. PANIC BUYING OF MEAT AND DAIRY PRODUCTS THROUGHOUT COUNTRY

_____

4. EDITORIAL   Perhaps this shows, in an extreme manner, what the environmentalists have been trying to tell us all along: Pollute your waters and you invite death.

_____

5. NEWS REPORT   All the quacks are selling remedies for what seems to be ailing everybody—special ointments, chemically treated soap, heavy doses of vitamin C, saunas, and daily jogging. But every reputable skin doctor I've spoken to says the same thing. "We don't know the cause, and we don't know the cure. The only thing that we are sure of is that everybody seems to have it!"

6. COMMENT   "At a time like this there are no poor, no rich, no commoners, no nobles; we are all united by the bond of unbearable tragedy."

7. TV DOCUMENTARY   "It's a combination of science fiction and fantasy. Thousands upon thousands of little green animals, coming at you from every direction."

WHAT THE TORAH SAYS*

Circle the letter before the statement that exactly completes the sentences below.

1. Pharaoh's continuing stubbornness in the face of Moses' pleas and warnings
   a. Showed that he did not scare easily.
   b. Proved how stupid he was.
   c. Was a result of his not wanting to lose face before the members of his court.
   d. Caused the Egyptian people great suffering.
   e. Demonstrated how much the Egyptian economy depended upon Hebrew slave labor.

2. After the Hebrew overseers rebuked Moses and Aaron for having made the Children of Israel "hateful in the eyes of Pharaoh," Moses
   a. Began to yearn for the life that he had known as a simple shepherd in Midian.
   b. Seriously quesioned the Lord's reasons for sending him on this mission, and the truth of His promise.
   c. Resented the overseers' bitter criticism of him.

89

    d. Felt guilty over the greater burdens that his actions had placed upon the Children of Israel.

    e. Realized that the Pharaoh was a tough opponent.

3. The lamb's blood on the lintel and doorposts of Israelite homes

    a. Caused Israelites and Egyptians both to worry.

    b. Looked ugly and grotesque, an omen of death.

    c. Insured that the people in those homes were not to be harmed.

    d. Placed the Children of Israel in greater danger than ever.

    e. Worried Moses, for he realized that if the Pharaoh did not respond to this plague, there was little hope for the Hebrew people.

4. The Ten Plagues

    a. Proved to Pharaoh the power of the Lord.

    b. Made the Egyptians hate the Children of Israel even more.

    c. Caused members of the royal court to doubt Pharaoh's wisdom.

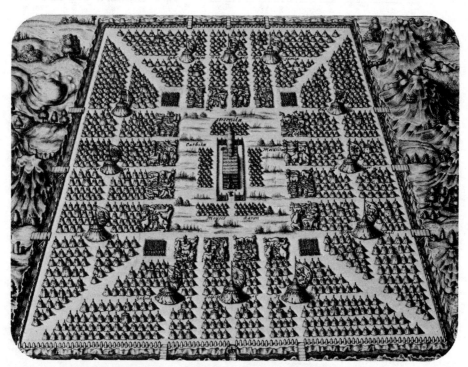

When the Israelites made camp in the wilderness, they grouped themselves by tribes and protected the Holy Ark by placing it in the center.

d. Gave Moses and Aaron increased prestige and respect in the eyes of both the Egyptians and the Children of Israel.

e. Stirred Pharaoh to do what Moses requested—at least while they were happening.

5. Pharaoh's first response to Moses' and Aaron's pleas might have been:

a. "The nerve of these people trying to tell me what to do!"

b. "If I do as they say, I show disrespect to the Egyptian gods."

c. "The best defense is an offense. When I am finished with them, they'll yearn for the 'good old days' and curse the coming of Moses and Aaron."

d. "Why can't they sacrifice to their so-called God right here? Why do they need to go into the wilderness? There's something fishy afoot!"

Midrash Review

LOOKING FOR UNDERSTANDING

How would you explain the following quotations from the Midrash?

1. "Even though Moses said he would speak in the name of the Lord, the elders furtively slipped away, one by one, as they approached the royal palace. Moses and Aaron appeared alone before the king." Midrash [1]

_____

_____

_____

2. "For fully twenty days before each plague, Moses warned the Egyptians of the affliction to come, in the hope that they would change their ways; but Pharaoh and his servants scoffed at the warnings." Midrash [5]

_____

_____

_____

3. "'What is your God's name?' the king answered calmly. 'Where does He live? How great is His strength? How many countries bow to Him? How many wars has He won?' " Midrash [2]

_____

_____

_____

4. " 'O Lord,' Moses cried, 'You sent me to rescue these people, but they suffer more than before! You sent me to save, and yet there is no redemption.' " Midrash [4]

_____

_____

_____

5. "Pharaoh replied angrily, 'I am a god, and I created myself. I cause the Nile to irrigate my land!' " Midrash [2]

_____

_____

_____

6. "Moses and Aaron declared that God rules over the entire earth, that the stars and planets are His creation, as well as the creatures of the world." Midrash [2]

_____

_____

_____

7. "He sent for the chronicles of Egypt, wherein were listed the gods of all the nations." Midrash [2]

_____

_____

_____

8. "God said,. . .'Moses, you must learn to be patient, and to understand that nothing of worth comes quickly. The Hebrews will

see My signs and learn My ways. Then will My purpose be revealed and will they become worthy of being redeemed.' " Midrash [4]

_____

_____

_____

SCRAMBLED TITLES*

This puzzle has three parts: first, unscramble the words; second, rearrange their order to make a logical title; third, apply that title to the Midrash that it best describes. (For example, **sredel het dworlacy** = elders the cowardly = the cowardly elders, which is one of the titles (there are others) that could be used to describe Midrash [1].)

1. **nia tafhi senols** = _____ =

   _____ = Midrash [   ]

2. **scat feedacin fo** = _____ =

   _____ = Midrash [   ]

3. **graconear tronbubs** = _____ =

   _____ = Midrash [   ]

4. **fo leurifa prasdelhei** = _____ =

   _____ = Midrash [   ]

Summing Up

THE MEANING OF LEADERSHIP

The role and meaning of leadership—that of Moses and Aaron, the elders of the Children of Israel, or the Pharaoh—is a major issue in this chapter. In Jewish life today, the question of leadership is no less important.

1. Complete the following sentences based on your view of Jewish life today:

   a. The major challenges facing the leaders of the American Jewish community are _____

   _____

   _____

   b. The major challenges facing Israeli leaders are_____

   _____

   _____

   c. A good American Jewish leader is one who _____

   _____

   _____

   d. A bad American Jewish leader is one who_____

   _____

   _____

2. Imagine that you are on a committee charged with the task of hiring a rabbi, an individual whose main job is promoting the well-being of your Jewish community. The following "excerpts" have been taken from letters of recommendation written about candidates for this job. Put a "1" beside the most important quality, in your opinion; a "2" beside the next most important; and so on.

   ____ "Very presentable-looking, and makes an excellent impression on Jew and non-Jew alike."
   ____ "A first-rate organizer, who knows how to motivate people and get them involved."
   ____ "A crackerjack fundraiser!"
   ____ "A dedicated educator, particularly interested in youth activities."

_____ "A brilliant scholar, who has written books about Jewish history and the Bible."

_____ "The word that best describes this person is 'mensch.' A person who listens, feels, understands—and above all, whom people come to talk to. One who does everything possible to help them!"

_____ "An ardent Zionist who is deeply aware of world Jewry, and committed to its well-being."

3. You are probably a member of one or more groups. In each of these groups, someone is a leader. If you were asked to make up a recipe, or a formula, for the best possible leader for your group, what would be the things you would look for? (Put the most important thing first.)

a. _____

b. _____

c. _____

d. _____

e. _____

4. Leadership, good or bad, is usually a question of people's values— those values that they consider most desirable. Let us imagine for a moment that personal qualities, and even experiences, are goods that can be purchased. You are the buyer, but with only a limited budget. How would you spread your money around? The following "merchandise" is for sale. Each item costs $33.33 ⅓. Bear in mind—in this little game, you only possess what you pay for; everything else is out of bounds. You have $100.00—now make your three choices.

a.	Physical beauty	$33.33 ⅓
b.	Popularity	$33.33 ⅓
c.	Brilliance	$33.33 ⅓
d.	Good health	$33.33 ⅓
e.	A sense of humor	$33.33 ⅓
f.	Good relationships with parents, husband or wife, and children	$33.33 ⅓
g.	Wealth and success	$33.33 ⅓
h.	Sensitivity, compassion, and generosity	$33.33 ⅓

i. Making a great contribution to humanity
(or to Judaism and the Jewish people) $33.33 ⅓

j. A powerful, unwavering belief in God throughout
your life $33.33 ⅓

Your choices:

1. _____

2. _____

3. _____

What do these choices tell you about yourself?

14 EXODUS [12-15]

THE EXODUS

Bible Review

FIND THE OUTSIDER*

In each of the following sentences, circle the letter before the section that does not belong.

1. Moses' declaration to the Children of Israel to "Fear not! Stand firm, and see how the Lord will save you today" shows that (a) the Children of Israel were frightened (b) the Egyptians were hated by the Lord (c) Moses had developed greatly as a leader, and as a man of faith, since the time of the burning bush in Midian (d) the Lord watched over the Children of Israel as they began their journey in the desert (e) the Children of Israel had not yet learned the meaning, and discipline, of faith.

2. The Children of Israel's statement to Moses, "Is it because there are no graves in Egypt that you have taken us away to die in the wilderness?. . . It would be better for us to serve the Egyptians than to die in the wilderness," teaches that (a) they still did not trust Moses' leadership, or his vision (b) they were not afraid to defy or criticize Moses openly (c) they had a sense of humor that could be very sarcastic on occasion (d) they had more faith in the Egyptian gods than they did in the One God (e) at this point, they preferred the security of slavery to the uncertainty, and danger, of freedom

3. The observance of Passover teaches us that (a) our ancestors were once slaves in the land of Egypt (b) our ancestors were forced to flee the land of bondage so quickly that they had no time to leaven their bread (c) if we believe in God and do as He tells us, we can never be harmed (d) God delivered the Children of

Israel from Egypt   (e) God affirmed His commitment to bring the Children of Israel to the land He promised to Abraham, Isaac, and Jacob   (f) we are obliged to convey the story and meaning of Passover to future generations of Jews

4. The parting of the waters of the Sea of Reeds showed   (a) the immensity of the Lord's power   (b) that those who do evil, and who defy the will of God, may be punished by death   (c) that God used the forces of nature to bring about His miracles   (d) that Moses was a kind of "middleman" between the Lord and His miracles   (e) that Moses was a wonder-worker of great ability

5. In "The Song of Moses,"   (a) God is given credit for saving the Children of Israel   (b) a curse is leveled at Egypt as a warning to future generations of oppressors   (c) the destruction of Pharaoh's army is dramatically described   (d) the power of the Lord is celebrated not only for the present, but for the future as well

LOOKING FOR UNDERSTANDING

Using the biblical text as your source, briefly answer the following questions in your own words:

1. Why did the Children of Israel take unleavened cakes of dough with them when they left Egypt?

   _____

   _____

   _____

2. Why did Moses take the bones of Joseph out of Egypt?

   _____

   _____

   _____

3. Why did Pharaoh and his servants set out in pursuit of the Children of Israel?

   _____

   _____

4. Why did the Children of Israel rebuke Moses when they saw the Egyptians coming after them?

_____

_____

5. Why did Moses command the Children of Israel, and their descendants for all time, to observe the holiday of Passover ("*Matzot* shall be eaten seven days. . . . You shall observe this ordinance in its season from year to year.")

_____

_____

Midrash Review

TRUE OR FALSE?*

Using the Midrash as your reference, answer the following:

1. After the Pharaoh witnessed the death of every Egyptian first-born child, he learned his lesson.   T [   ]   F [   ]

2. Among those who were part of the Exodus from Egypt were Egyptians as well as Hebrews.   T [   ]   F [   ]

3. Moses understood that courage and faith were qualities that had to be taught and developed, often slowly.   T [   ]   F [   ]

4. The Pharaoh's greed, stupidity, and stubbornness brought a great deal of unnecessary suffering to his people.   T [   ]   F [   ]

5. After the destruction of the Pharaoh's army in the Sea of Reeds, Egyptian memory of, and bitterness toward, the Children of Israel all but disappeared.   T [   ]   F [   ]

LESSONS FROM THE MIDRASH

Identify the particular Midrash (by number) in which the following attitudes and ideas are expressed. If a lesson is set forth in more than one

Midrash (or if a Midrash contains more than one lesson), there is room for more than one number in the brackets below.

1. True faith does not merely mean bearing calm witness to magic and miracles; it demands courage—to walk into the realm of the unknown, fully aware of the uncertainties and dangers that may be awaiting. Midrash [   ]

2. Punishment, with its accompanying pain, can cloud and con – fuse the mind of the sufferer, rather than clarify matters. Midrash [   ]

3. There is a time for thought and prayer, and a time for action. Midrash [   ]

4. God does not require gifts, or taxes, or other forms of tribute. That form of homage is contrary to His nature. Midrash [   ]

5. There are many ways of measuring value and finding one's responsibilities. Midrash [   ]

Summing Up

COMMUNICATION

Imagine that you have a non-Jewish pen pal who is very curious about Passover, and wants to know as much as possible about its meaning. You explain that the reason for observing this holiday is to remember the various lessons learned from the experience of the Exodus. Your pen pal replies, "What *are* these lessons?" How would you answer this question?

A MAP OF THE SEDER TABLE

Passover is a holiday with many symbols that remind us of the way things were in the days of Moses, and the lessons that we must teach from generation to generation. The following "map" shows objects that are placed upon the traditional Seder table. In the space above the lines pointing to each object, identify the item in question; in the space below, briefly explain what it stands for.

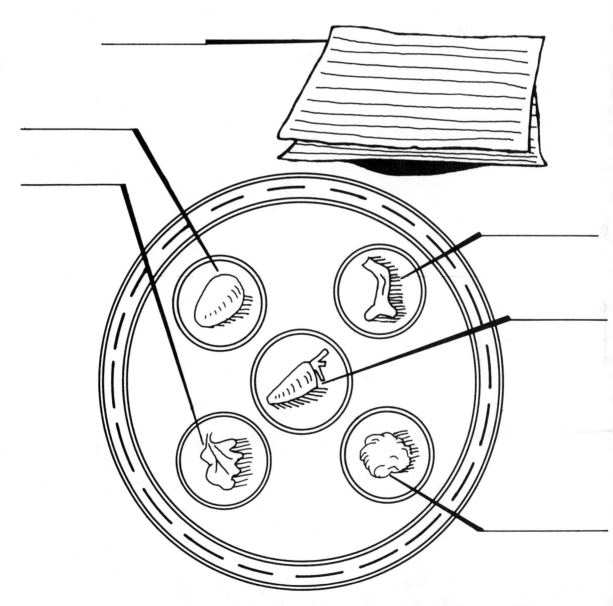

ANSWER KEY

This workbook has two kinds of questions: those which may be answered by reference to facts and data in the textbook; and those which require the students to interpret the material being studied in the light of his or her own ideas. The following Key provides answers *only* for those questions that are factual in nature.

Chapter One

SCENES OF THE CREATION (page 1)

A. Fifth day   B. Third day   C. First day   D. Sixth day   E. Fourth day   F. The Sabbath   G. Second day   H. Fifth day   I. Sixth day   J. Third day

TRUE OR FALSE? (page 2)

1. True   2. False   3. False   4. True   5. False   6. False   7. False   8. True   9. True   10. False   11. False   12. True

WORD SCRAMBLE (page 3)

1. Tree   2. Fruit   3. Serpent   4. Knowledge   5. Shame
Circled letters: Punishment

FIND THE OUTSIDER (page 3)

1. e   2. b   3. d   4. b   5. c

Chapter Two

WHO (OR WHAT) AM I? (page 7)

1. The rainbow   2. The Tower of Babel   3. Cain's offering   4. Seth
5. The dove   6. The mark of Cain   7. Noah   8. Abel
9. Noah's ark   10. The flood

WHAT THE TORAH SAYS (page 8)

1. (d)   2. (c)   3. (b)   4. (b)   5. (d)   6. (e)   7. (c)   8. (d)

BETWEEN THE LINES (page 9)

3;   4;   6;   1;   2;   5

Chapter Three

FINDING THE FACTS (page 17)

Sarai; Lot; Ur; Chaldees; Canaan; Haran; nation;
Shechem; Altar; quarrels; separate; Jordan; well
watered; sins; walked; Mamre; Hebron; four kings; share;
childless; Eliezer; born; stars; covenant; Hagar; Ishmael

MAP STUDY: ABRAM'S JOURNEYS (page 18)

1. Shechem   2. Ur of the chaldees   3. Egypt   4. Salt Sea (popularly
known as the Dead Sea)   5. Haran   6. The Negev   7. Dan
8. Mamre, in Hebron   9. The plain of the Jordan

Chapter Four

TRUE OR FALSE? (page 25)

1. False   2. False   3. True   4. False   5. True   6. True   7. False
8. True   9. False   10. True

A RECIPE FOR DESTRUCTION (page 28)

1. greed   2. violence   3. cruelty to strangers   4. oppression of the poor
5. unjust laws

ABRAHAM'S JOURNAL (page 28)

7;   6;   8;   1;   10;   9;   2;   5;   3;   4

Chapter Five

FIND THE OUTSIDER (page 33)

1. d   2. b   3. c   4. e   5. a

WHO, WHAT, OR WHERE? (page 34)

1. Hebron   2. The ram   3. Moriah   4. The angel of the Lord
5. Ephron the Hittite   6. Machpelah

MAP STUDY: AN OLD-NEW LAND (page 37)

1. Beer-sheba   2. Hebron   3. Moriah   4. Sodom   5. Salt Sea
(Dead Sea)

Chapter Six

WORD SCRAMBLE (page 43)

1. Beauty   2. Generosity   3. Compassion   4. Courage   5. Healer
Circled letters: Righteousness

ELIEZER's NOTEBOOK (page 46)

1. Abram's smashing Terah's idols   2. The departure from Haran for Canaan   3. Abram's rescuing Lot   4. The birth of Ishmael 5. The binding of Isaac   6. Abram and Sarai are given new names by the Lord   7. God's rebuke of Abraham for his treatment of his pagan guest   8. The birth of Isaac   9. The destruction of Sodom and Gomorrah   10. Eliezer's encounter with Rebekah at the well

Chapter Seven

WHAT THE TORAH SAYS (page 48)

1. d   2. c   3. b   4. e   5. a   6. d

TRUE OR FALSE? (page 49)

1. False   2. True   3. True   4. True   5. False   6. False   7. True
8. True   9. True   10. False   11. True   12. False

Chapter Eight

JACOB'S MAP (page 54)

A. Beer-sheba   B. Beth-el   C. Haran   D. The Jordan River
E. Bethlehem   F. Mamre (in Hebron)

IF IT HAPPENED TODAY (page 54)

1. Laban   2. Jacob   3. Leah   4. Esau   5. Laban   6. Israel (Jacob)
7. Isaac

NAMES AND THEIR MEANINGS (page 59)

4;   8;   9;   6;   1;   10;   3;   5;   2;   7

Chapter Nine

FILL IN THE BLANKS (page 60)

resented; favored; fuel; squealer; serve; annoy; hostility; instincts; Egypt

WHO SAID WHAT? (page 60)

1. Pharaoh's cupbearer   2. Jacob   3. Potiphar's wife   4. Judah
5. Pharaoh   6. Pharaoh's baker   7. Jacob   8. Potiphar

FIND THE OUTSIDER (page 62)

1. b   2. d   3. c   4. e   5. a

WHAT MADE THEM DO IT? (page 65)

3;   4;   5;   1;   2

Chapter Ten

NEWS HEADLINES (page 66)

1. Joseph's first meeting with his brothers in Egypt

2. Jacob's response to the proposal that Benjamin be sent to Egypt to prove that the brothers are not spies, and to insure Simeon's release

3. The brothers find their money in the sacks with the grain they received from Joseph

4. Jacob agrees to send Benjamin to Egypt

5. Judah asks Joseph to keep him as hostage and to release Benjamin

6. Joseph's statement to his brothers after admitting to them his real identity

TRUE OR FALSE? (page 67)

1. False   2. True   3. True   4. False   5. False   6. False   7. True
8. True   9. False   10. True

Chapter Eleven

LEAVES FROM A REPORTER'S NOTEBOOK (page 72)

alive; gratitude; gifts; the land of Canaan; a vision; deep emotion; good will; positions of responsibility; a blessing; prospered and multiplied; renewed his commitment; confused and disturbed; in reverse order; view of the future; Ephraim; greater nation; stilled their fears; bitterness; revenge

WHAT THE TORAH SAYS (page 74)

1. e   2. c   3. d   4. b   5. e   6. c   7. e

Chapter Twelve

A ROUND ROBIN REVIEW (page 79)

1a. Jethro   1b. Midianite priest   1c. Midwife   1d. Pithom and Raamses   1e. Zipporah   1f. Mount Horeb   1g. Aaron   1h. Levi

2a. True   2b. True   2c. False   2d. False   2e. True   2f. True   2g. False   2h. True

4. f;   d;   e;   b;   a;   c;

5a. 3   5b. 4   5c. 1   5d. 5

MAP STUDY (page 86)

1. Goshen   2. The Nile River   3. Pithom and Raamses   4. Midian   5. Mount Horeb

Chapter Thirteen

A MEDIA MIX (page 88)

1. ninth plague: darkness   2. seventh plague: thunder and hail   3. fifth plague: the death of Pharaoh's cattle   4. first plague: waters turn to blood   5. sixth plague: boils   6. tenth plague: death of the Egyptian firstborn children   7. second plague: frogs

WHAT THE TORAH SAYS (page 89)

1. d   2. b   3. c   4. e   5. c

SCRAMBLED TITLES (page 93)

1. A Lesson in Faith, Midrash [4]   2. Acts of Defiance, Midrash [3]
3. Stubborn Arrogance, Midrash [2]   4. Failure of Leadership,
Midrash [1]

Chapter Fourteen

FIND THE OUTSIDER (page 97)

1. b   2. d   3. c   4. e   5. b

TRUE OR FALSE? (page 99)

1. False   2. True   3. True   4. True   5. False